# Are You Killing Your Relationships?

Men and women share a common problem that can be fatal to good relating. That problem—selfishness—is the central obstacle to developing good marriages and friendships. But you can breathe new life into your relationships with members of the opposite sex with Dr. Larry Crabb's unique approach to relating and his straightforward guidelines for improving communication between men and women.

Drawing on years of counseling experience, as well as faith in and guidance from the Scripture, Dr. Crabb explains the importance of turning self-centeredness into other-centeredness, while he outlines the steps necessary to achieve that end. With the help of Dr. Crabb's insightful and inspirational lessons, anyone can confidently restore harmony to a suffering relationship.

## Other books by **Dr. Larry Crabb**

*Basic Principles of Biblical Counseling*

*Effective Biblical Counseling*

*How to Become One with Your Mate*

*Understanding People: Deep Longings for Relationship*

*Encouragement: The Key to Caring* (with Dan Allender)

*The Marriage Builder*

*Inside Out*

# Men

♂ & ♀

# Women

## ENJOYING THE
## DIFFERENCE

## Dr. Larry Crabb

HarperPaperbacks
ZondervanPublishingHouse
*Divisions of HarperCollinsPublishers*

Published in association with literary agent, Sealy M. Yates, Orange, California.

All Scripture quotations, unless otherwise indicated, are taken from the Holy Bible: New International Version (North American Edition). Copyright © 1973, 1978, 1984 by the International Bible Society. Used by permission of Zondervan Bible Publishers.

HarperPaperbacks    *A Division of* HarperCollins*Publishers*
10 East 53rd Street, New York, N.Y. 10022

A hardcover edition of this book was published in 1991 by Zondervan Publishing House.

First HarperPaperbacks printing: December 1994

Printed in the United States of America

HarperPaperbacks and colophon are trademarks of HarperCollins*Publishers*

❖ 10 9 8 7 6 5 4 3

**To Rachael**

*More than anyone else she has helped me to ponder, value, and enjoy the differences*

# Contents

Foreword                                    ix
Preface                                     xi
Acknowledgments                             xiii
Introduction                                xv

*Part One*
Why Relationships Don't Work:
The Problem Men and Women Share

*One*
What's Wrong with Our Marriage?             3

*Two*
Facing Ourselves Honestly                   18

*Three*
The Real Problem                            38

*Four*
Surely I'm Not That Bad!                     54

*Five*
Change is Possible                          70

*Six*
Celebrating Forgiveness                     90

*Part Two*
How Relationships Do Work:
The Difference Men and Women Can Enjoy

*Seven*
A Tough Question                                   109

*Eight*
Is There Really a Difference?                       121

*Nine*
Masculinity and Femininity                          143

*Ten*
Unique Ways to Freely Love                          159

*Eleven*
Relating as Men and Women                           182

*Twelve*
Enjoying the Difference                             196

Notes                                               215

# Foreword

*Marriage in America sometimes resembles business —* lean and leveraged. For many, marrying is little more than a credit risk or a friendly takeover. Expectations of short-term benefits, no-load advantages, and good diversity crouch in the hidden agenda. The "smart money" moves toward keeping control, staying on top, buying low, and selling high.

Christian marriage, however, embraces no such safety nets, no fine-print exclusions, no white knights. The only prenuptial agreement God requires is that he, the Designer, be consulted. His warranty rests on the God-Husband-Wife triangle — a joint venture. Each flows into and out of the other, and the net profit is mutual enjoyment.

More than four decades ago we stood in a small church and publicly pledged lifelong commitment to each other. It was a step of faith, for we didn't really know each other well. More strategically, we didn't know ourselves. To borrow again from the business world, we immediately began to spend each other. The security of having a lifetime partner raised us, emotionally speaking, to a higher-income group. We found ourselves using up our savings. In the words of Paul, we were "biting and devouring each another," in danger of destroying ourselves.

Like many marriages, ours developed unseen

leaks, easily hidden by busyness and cover-ups. Of course we were in love, trying to remain emotionally solvent, but time and again we came up short and didn't understand why.

Dr. Larry Crabb has audited many marriages just like our early one. He has identified the real culprit—the self we bring to the marriage altar. Self-centeredness, he reminds us, snarls our marital budget. It is the "sin which so easily besets." Until we red-flag our pet liabilities, especially anger, and replace it with forgiveness, the deficits will mount.

Out of his years of counseling experience, Dr. Crabb warns that it is not enough to come out even: marriage is a joyous union in which self-sacrifice is to be celebrated. When we put the other person first with no thought of being repaid, gladness and fulfillment will be God's dividends. The gains of marriage are paid out particularly as we celebrate our sexual differences; each partner enriches the relationship to make it a daring adventure.

Of all the information and statistics published to make marriages more meaningful, this "report and recommendation" soars over most of them because of its biblical balance and real-life solutions. For men and women who want to invest in a profitable marriage, here is a guide to the bottom line of beauty and lifetime benefits.

HOWARD AND JEANNE HENDRICKS
CENTER FOR CHRISTIAN LEADERSHIP
DALLAS THEOLOGICAL SEMINARY

# Preface

*Two trends in the Christian world disturb me. First, the* gospel is gradually being reduced to the message that Christ provides us with a new identity to replace the damaged one we acquired from being raised in dysfunctional families. Second, our identity in Christ is commonly being interpreted in a way that hides our uniqueness as men and women beneath our equality as Christians.

The older I get, the more I cling passionately to a handful of truths that seem increasingly important and that seem to directly contradict these two trends.

One of those truths is that the beginning of the gospel is the message of judgment, but its central jewel is forgiveness. Unless we recognize how deep is our sin and how wonderful Christ's forgiveness, we will pervert the truth of our identity in Christ into the worthless bauble of preoccupying self-love. But if we realize that forgiveness is the showcase of God's grace, then we will learn the joys of our new identity by devoting ourselves to worshiping God and serving others.

A second truth is this: when our identity is legitimately affirmed, we will become more distinctively masculine and feminine in all of our relationships. We will be eager to give what our sexuality equips us to give with the well-being of others in mind rather than that of ourselves.

This book revolves around these two beliefs, which directly compete with the two trends I've already mentioned. I hope that this book prompts dialogue among both those who support the trends and those who oppose them. For me, the idea that the gospel centers on the wonder of ongoing forgiveness and the view that men and women, although equally redeemed and equal heirs, are enjoyably different at their core both fall into the category of "things I have learned and become convinced of."

# Acknowledgments

*A number of people have significantly contributed to the* development of my ideas and to getting them into readable form.

My editor, Sandy Vander Zicht, challenged me to think hard, critique other views carefully, and express myself clearly. We don't always agree, but we work well together. Her commitment to seeing my ideas effectively communicated has added greatly to whatever merit the book may have.

My literary agent, Sealy Yates, has become both a trusted advisor and a close friend; he has freed me to do what I do well by conscientiously doing what he does well on my behalf.

The staff of Tyndale House in Cambridge, England, especially Dr. Bruce Winters, provided my wife and me with three of the best months of my life, a time to write and think in the enjoyably stimulating atmosphere of a Christian study center.

Special thanks to a special friend, Judy Primeaux, who actually wanted to decipher my handwritten pages and type the manuscript, and who did so in between the cracks of a busy life because she believed in me and wanted to think through what I had to say. Thanks, Judy!

I cannot imagine working on a major project without depending heavily on several individuals: Dr. Dan Allender, my colleague of fifteen years and a much loved and highly respected friend; Dr.

Tom Varney, a more recent colleague whose input is always supportive and insightful; Dr. Bill Crabb, my brother and fellow psychologist who offered dozens of helpful suggestions on the manuscript; my parents, Larry, Sr., and Isabel Crabb, whose marriage of more than fifty years is my primary model for what it means to live happily together as man and woman; my staff (Lori Wheeler, Sue Rike, Cheryl Jones, and Natalie Merilatt), who wonderfully encourage me in so many ways.

My deepest thanks and love to Rachael, my wife of almost twenty-five years who has taught me more than anyone about how to enjoy the differences between a man and woman. I have the privilege of enjoying her uniqueness every day.

The list is long. My gratitude is sincere. I do, of course, accept full responsibility for the ideas expressed in this book.

# Introduction

*A recent letter to Ann Landers[1] began* "I am 19 and have made the decision not to marry. Why am I so cynical? Let me explain."

The writer goes on to describe several miserable marriages in her extended family. Referring to great-aunts, grandmothers, and cousins after their husbands had died, she observed that "for every woman in our family who was genuinely saddened by her husband's death, five blossomed, smiled more and did more interesting and exciting things. The quality of their lives was greatly improved, and it is obvious that they love widowhood."

How tragic when the death of a spouse provokes more of a sense of relief than loss!

The disillusioned teenager ended her letter with a comment that reveals more about the roots of her cynicism than she perhaps understood or intended: "My father is a grim, stern, joyless person, and I'm pretty sure that my mother will enjoy life much more after he goes."

I wish that such cynical attitudes about marriage were rare. But in response to the nineteen-year-old's letter, Ann Landers received "hundreds of letters" from women stuck in unrewarding marriages, two of which she published in a subsequent column.[2] And more and more people of all ages report that their exposure to marriage, including their own, does not encourage a confidence that years of living together will produce the joys of intimate relationship all of us want. Too often, what passes for a good marriage is a routine, pleasant arrangement that avoids loneliness and keeps things predictable and safe.

A closer look beneath the thin veneer of social courtesy often reveals tension, bickering, and rage that threaten to shatter any hope of harmony, and we are hard put to find couples who would make a good advertisement for marriage as a thrilling opportunity for warm, satisfying companionship and meaningful intimacy in an uncaring world.

None of us is immune to the spirit of cynicism. As I recently watched two good friends exchange vows, I couldn't help wondering, for at least a moment, if they would have what it takes to nurture a truly good relationship. Would they be able to successfully work through the strains that inevitably develop when two imperfect people carrying baggage from their past link their lives together? I'm not sure. I never am. I know that very few couples escape those terrible times when anger is intense, divorce seems attractive, and hopes for enjoying each other seem unrealistic.

When I notice the eager smiles of the bride and groom as they turn to face life together as Mr. and Mrs., I sometimes think of the hundreds of couples I've counseled who smiled just as broadly on their wedding day but who now have little reason to rejoice. The honeymoon has ended, and they're bored, irritable, desperate, or comfortably detached from one another in a passionless routine that neither partner has the energy to break.

What does it take to build a good marriage? Is it really possible? With all the attention we have given to understanding relationships, have we learned anything about what is required to develop a closeness that deepens with time, or are we moving away from the understanding we need? We do not lack ideas about communication, commitment, self-understanding, and personal growth; so it seems the picture should be brightening. But it's not.

As I reflect on ongoing struggles with marriage and think hard about biblical teaching on who we are and what's wrong with us, it seems to me that our culture addresses secondary problems as though they were central and, in the process of energetically dealing with those problems, overlooks the real killer of relationships.

Sometimes we labor so carefully to define proper roles for husbands and wives that we produce a pharisaical code of conduct that gives birth to stiffly courteous relationships. Other times we emphasize so strongly the importance of learning to like ourselves and focus so intently on repairing the damage to our "self" inflicted on us by a rejecting, insensitive, and sometimes brutal world, that "fixing ourselves" becomes more important than "giving ourselves." We replace stiff courtesy with self-absorbed vulnerability that fails to produce intimacy.

Either we try hard to do better, thinking that the problem is lack of discipline and effort, or we work to develop ourselves, hoping to overcome the self-hatred and feelings of emptiness that we assume are the real culprits getting in the way of good relating. But neither approach replaces an overriding commitment to our own well-being with a humble, freely chosen concern for the well-being of others. Neither approach leads to our becoming the giving men and women we were designed to be.

Something is missing in our efforts to build good marital relationships. Perhaps a *fundamental flaw* in the way we try to create intimacy must be corrected before any other attempts to improve things will have effect. And perhaps this flaw has something to do with our having lost the uniqueness of what it means to relate to one another as *men* and *women*. Maybe cramming people into tightly defined roles according to gender has stifled the appropriate expression of our sexuality. On the other hand, maybe emphasizing that men and women are equal in worth, in redemption, and in capacity for service has blurred legitimate distinctions in the way we were designed to relate to one another, distinctions that should be enjoyed, not dismissed as outdated.

I wrote this book in an effort to think through one central question: *What can a man and woman bring to a marriage that, more than anything else, will create a relationship that gets better with time?* Or, to put it more simply, what does it take to make a marriage work?

If we can answer this question, then perhaps we will be able to face honestly what is happening in marriages today with the confidence that married couples can realize the potential for intimacy and with the hope that marriage — two becoming one — will be cause for celebration, not cynicism.

# Men
# &
# Women

# *Part One*

## Why Relationships Don't Work: The Problem Men and Women Share

# One

## What's Wrong with Our Marriage?

*"Original sin" means we all originate out of a sinful world which taints us from the word go. We all tend to make ourselves the center of the universe.*

FREDERICK BUECHNER

*Listen to these comments I've recently heard from four* individuals, each in a different troubled marriage.

*Wife A:* "It's gotten to the point where I can't take any more. I've got to start thinking of myself. I'm totally unhappy as his wife."

*Husband B:* "After twenty-six years of no affection, I've had it. If just once she would warmly reach over and show an interest in giving me pleasure, I could stick it out."

*Wife C:* "I just don't feel alive anymore. Somewhere along the line I died. He thinks that the only reason I exist is to supply him with food, sex, and clean shirts. I've got to break out of this coffin."

*Husband D:* "I'm not sure why, but life doesn't mean much anymore. I love my wife, but not the way I used to. The spark just isn't there. Everything seems so boring. There's got to be more to life than this."

No one would quarrel with the observation that these folks are hurting. Each one is feeling real pain. They are angry, scared, empty, frustrated, and sometimes desperate.

Most caring people would want to find some way to relieve their pain, to give immediate attention to their wounded hearts.

Many counselors would agree. The most important thing to do is to heal their wounds: Build up self-images, uncover dynamic forces within personalities that block the free expression of identity, break patterns of co-dependency, help people erect boundaries between themselves and others that protect them from negative influences and provide them with enough space to grow. A thousand strategies exist for helping people feel better about themselves.

But notice something else, something that seems almost unkind to point out, something so terribly obvious that we might pass right over it. The four spouses regard their hurt as the most important problem. *They are committed, first of all, to themselves.*

Each one, without blushing, holds fast to an overriding concern for his or her own well-being. Other things may matter, but nothing matters more than their own happiness and personal satisfaction.

When I talked with these four men and women, it became clear that not one thought of his or her self-centeredness as a serious problem. When each thought about this commitment to self at all, it seemed not only as natural as breathing, but entirely justified.

What is *wrong* with these wives and husbands, and countless others like them, who know very little of the enjoyment marriage is supposed to provide? Is the core problem the personal damage that patterns of poor relating have produced? Are they wounded victims in need of healing? Or is there a problem within that is worse than whatever wounds they carry? Is there a self-interest that is *not* healthy and normal but destructive and wrong?

There is, of course, legitimate self-interest. When I order my meal from a restaurant menu, I choose food I want to eat. I'm thinking about myself. Choosing items I don't like (disgusting things like lima beans or sweet potatoes) would show not mature self-denial, but a lapse in sensible living. It is not wrong to indulge our taste buds, for our sakes alone. Similarly, it is not selfish to marry someone whom we expect to enjoy. To do otherwise is foolish.

Desiring our own good is not sinful in itself, but natural and instinctive. God gave us everything, even our very existence. He wants us to take care of what he gave us. It is the act of putting ourselves at the center of the universe, where God belongs, that is unqualified sin. This is, in fact, the very definition of sin.

When self-interest continues as the dominant commitment of our lives, when we devote our energy to serving ourselves above all others, then we are wrongly self-centered. And this form of self-interest is a far more serious and dangerous problem than the wounds we suffer at the hands of others.

But very few people even notice their commitment to self-interest, and among those who do, even fewer are deeply concerned about it. More often, self-centeredness is encouraged: "Look out for yourself. Who else is going to?" "You shouldn't have to put up with that kind of treatment." "You must learn to take care of yourself before you can properly give to others."

All relationships, even the best ones, have hard, disappointing moments. And when we are treated unfairly, an energetic determination to recover some measure of personal comfort seems reasonable and thoroughly justified. Nothing is more natural, especially when we suffer from wounds caused by unjust treatment from another, than to regard our *immediate well-being as the final purpose justice should serve.*

People are *wounded*, and people are *self-centered*. We must decide which is the greater problem.

The wounds of men, in some ways, are different from the wounds of women. In marriage, men complain more of sexual frustration, and women hurt more over the lack of sensitive involvement. Differences like these need to be explored and understood to help us give more meaningfully to one another. But neither men nor women are naturally inclined to give of themselves on behalf of others. Those who rightly insist on the equality of both sexes would do well to begin by insisting that men and women are *equally fallen* and are therefore equally committed to advancing their own interest. Whatever our similarities and differences, men and women are bound up in a self-centered approach to life that can be dislodged only by an ongoing encounter with a forgiving and gracious God.

We will not move very far in our efforts to develop good marriages until we understand that repairing a damaged sense of identity and healing the wound in our hearts is *not* the first order of business. It is rather dealing with the subtle, pervasive, stubborn commitment to ourselves.

Self-centeredness is the killer. In every bad relationship, it is the deadliest culprit. Poor communication, temper problems, unhealthy responses to dysfunctional family backgrounds, co-dependent relationships, and personal incompatibility— everything (unless medically caused) flows out of the cesspool of self-centeredness.

Before we can begin to talk about putting marriages together, before we can properly discuss the differences between men and women and how they can be enjoyed, before we can recover from our wounds, we must deal with our common problem of self-centeredness in a way that transforms us more and more into *other-centered* people.

## TWO WAYS OF THINKING

In Christian circles, two popular approaches to building relationships exist. Though they are different, each moves us away from correcting our deep problem of self-centeredness. The *first approach* insists that suffering is such an unthinkable violation of a person's dignity that nothing matters more than healing wounds and restoring identity. Woundedness is treated as a far more urgent problem than self-centeredness.

The *second approach* clubs hurting people over the head with biblical standards in a way that drives them *not* to Christ and to selfless living, but rather to frustration when they fail or pride when they think they don't. Those holding to this way of thinking reduce self-centeredness to acts of blatant sinfulness that can be cured by exhortations and scoldings. They hammer against sin, superficially defined, with an insensitivity to hurt and pain.

The first way of thinking regards *wounds* from unjust treatment as a far more significant problem than self-centeredness. The second, in its pressured demands to do what's right, contemptuously ignores deep hurt. Neither humanists who put self-development at the center of everything, nor pharisees who self-righteously enforce the law provide much help in putting joy back into marriage.

## Self-Development

Consider the counsel that advocates of the first approach, where self-development is key, might offer the four hurting, self-committed spouses mentioned at the beginning of this chapter.

> *Response to Wife A:* "Let's explore your pain and see what can be done to relieve it."
>
> *Response to Husband B:* "I wonder if you've felt starved for affection for a long time. Perhaps your strong response to your wife's coldness reflects a deep insecurity that we could work on."
>
> *Response to Wife C:* "Certainly there's more to you than cook, sex partner, and wash woman. Maybe you've been afraid to be who you really are for fear no one would want you. Perhaps as you learn to develop neglected parts of your personality, your husband will

come to see you as more than a useful
object. Even if he doesn't, you'll be happier
with yourself."

*Response to Husband D:* "You seem scared to venture out in new directions. Your boredom
may be the result of a poor self-image that
keeps you from trying new things and taking risks, both with your wife and in business."

These responses reflect the idea that an empty,
restricted, dull self is the central problem. Self-
development is the answer. God is regarded as the
great source of vitality, as the liberator who rips
off the chains of self-restriction to permit the full
expression of our humanness. Because of the
cross, in this way of thinking, we can seize opportunities to live out our potential and risk the rejection of others. The death of Christ becomes a balm
for wounds and a platform on which to build identity rather than an atonement for sin.

Self-centeredness is set aside as a lesser problem.
Self-development, and the liberty that comes when
people feel more alive, is the real need. Like most
bad ideas, this one probably developed in reaction
to an opposite but equally wrong viewpoint, one
that deals no more effectively with the real problem of self-centeredness.

## Moral Restraint

In conservative circles, Christianity too often
has been reduced to a joyless moralism, a set of
responsibilities that need to be obeyed to demonstrate a regenerated heart. Unlike those adhering
to the first view, which presents Christianity as a

chance to come alive as a person, those holding to this second view typically talk about duties and commandments. Moralists would respond differently to the four hurting spouses:

*Response to Wife A:* "I'm sure it's hard to continue living with someone as mean as your husband. But God requires you to do so—and he never commands without providing enablement."

*Response to Husband B:* "Your wife's lack of affection may be difficult to handle, but it's no excuse for leaving her."

*Response to Wife C:* "It's regrettable that you feel so used and empty. But your role as a wife is to submit to your husband—and knowing that you are obeying God will be your joy."

*Response to Husband D:* "Whether the spark is there or not, God commands you to love your wife. Remember, love is not a feeling. Loving your wife is a decision to be good to her followed by action. Do what love demands."

Although there is much that is correct and good in these responses, there may be also a joy-killing, legalistic attitude that goes something like this: "You are not free to enjoy the grace of God until your behavior demonstrates your commitment."

The heart of legalism makes required performance more central to Christian living than our Lord's invitation to enjoy him. In this view, the Lord's death becomes the basis for pressured living; introduces us to a list of rules spelled out by church authorities who never seem to see people as persons—persons who hurt, cry, feel lonely, and remember horrible things done to them in the middle of the night when they were children.

For legalists, words like *authenticity* and *personhood* have little place. Instead, words like *authority* and *obedience* are wrongly used to enforce rigid conformity to imposed standards; conformity is then regarded as holy living. Holiness is *rightly* seen as an issue more fundamental than self-expression, but is *wrongly* defined to mean "do right things" rather than "love God and others."

People who measure holiness solely by externals give little thought to what may be going on in the heart. Passion and joy are lost and grace is obscured when obedience to biblical standards is taught in a way that pressures people to do right to gain God's acceptance.

Rather than relating to God as *persons* who have been forgiven and called to a life of fullness and meaning, legalists try to fit people into boxes. Those who fit (can it be that some think they do?) feel proud. Those who fail wonder why they cannot be as spiritual as everyone else.

In the cold climate of legalism where sermons feel like spankings, it's not hard to understand the eager reception given to the idea that freedom means the chance to come alive, to repair internal damage, to face your struggles honestly and do something about them, to think about who *you* are for a change, to go after what *you* want and to express *your* talents, opinions, and feelings. The shift from harsh spankings to false encouragement is welcomed by many. Self-development is a more appealing value than pressured morality.

## DAMAGE TO MARRIAGE

With its insistence on living by rigid rules and functioning within narrow roles, moralistic Christianity has done real damage. And nowhere has the damage been greater than in marriage.

In the name of submission, wives have endured every imaginable form of abuse. They worry that God requires them to sit still while their husbands beat them; they push themselves to cooperate sexually even when exhausted to avoid God's displeasure and their husbands' scorn.

Many have lived within the narrow limits of what women are permitted to do, restrictions supported more often by masculine egos than by clear scriptural teaching. And their lives have been tragically emptied of meaning and joy. A Christianity that emphasizes rule-keeping over relationship cannot tolerate ambiguity or freedom, especially when it comes to a wife's responsibilities.

Far more often than most suspect, men have twisted biblical teaching on headship to justify dominating their wives, in some cases literally ordering them about as a master would a dog. Headship, a principle derived from Ephesians 5, is traditionally understood to mean that the husband should assume leadership in the home and the church. Yet biblical teaching never indulges the sinful human tendency to lead as a power-hungry despot. Should a wife really "fetch" a cup of coffee when the signal is given? Husbands who would never think to wash their wives' feet (much less the family's dishes) or to respect their wives' opinions enough to be guided by them have little understanding of either servant leadership or their own arrogance.

Moralism also damages men, but in a different way. Many husbands have crumbled under the weight of wrong perceptions about husbanding, knowing that they simply are not as strong or as wise as they think they should be. Sometimes defeated men have turned to pornography, adultery, depression, and workaholism to find relief from the intolerable burden to be more than they are. Adultery clearly is wrong. And so is the demand for relief that fuels it. But the pressure to meet false standards can be so intense that whatever provides relief seems justified.

## WE NEED NEW THINKING

If this brand of Christianity is traditional, and in too many circles it is, then we need new thinking that is as old as the Bible itself. We need to go deeper than a *moralistic* understanding of sin to grasp what the essence of sin looks like. We need to see how *a commitment to the self* operates when bad things inflict deep wounds in our souls, how we work to preserve some sense of our integrity when we come up against a damaging world, how enraged we become at others who hurt us and at a God who cannot be trusted to protect us from the severe wounds that life can inflict, and what we do with that rage. We need to respond with compassion and sensitivity to our wounds while at the same time recognizing the more central problem of self-centeredness.

Let me explain by giving an illustration. I was in Pittsburgh speaking to a church group on building relationships. After I had completed one of my lectures, a woman in brown slacks and a flowered blouse approached me.

"Dr. Crabb, I really appreciated what you had to say about establishing solid relationships," she said. "But I have a real problem. No matter how nice someone is to me, I can't keep myself from wondering if they really like me. I feel like they might turn on me at any moment."

I asked her whether she had any idea why she reacted this way. In response, she told me a tragic story.

This woman had been raised by parents whom I can only describe as unspeakably evil. From the time she was five years old until she was ten, her father sold her to the landlord every month in exchange for free rent. Each time her father drove her to the landlord's house, knowing that his daughter would be subjected to perverted sexual acts, he would warmly express his love and appreciation for the "help" she was providing the family.

While I was still reeling from this story, she told me about another incident.

When she was about three years old, she discovered an old-fashioned heating duct in the floor of her second-floor bedroom. This duct opened directly into the ceiling of the living room below, and by lying flat on the floor with her face pressed against the iron grate, she could look down into the living room without anyone knowing it.

A few days before Christmas, she used her newly discovered peephole to watch her parents wrap Christmas gifts in the room below. She was so happy and excited, dreaming of dolls and toys and pretty clothes, that she never noticed her mother leave the room.

Suddenly she heard footsteps behind her, and there was her mother, standing in the bedroom doorway watching her. Rather than enjoying her daughter's pleasure in peeking and chiding her lovingly to wait for Santa Claus to come in a few days, the mother burst into a rage. She grabbed the child, yanked off the heating vent, pulled the grate up, and stuffed her into the duct. She replaced the grate and left the little girl in that duct for three days.

When I heard these tales of horror, my immediate reaction was to wish this woman's parents were within reach. I wanted to punch them, strangle them, and beat their heads against a wall until they bled. Even now I don't feel terribly apologetic for this reaction.

Through no fault of her own, this woman had been a victim of unspeakable evil. She needed encouragement, compassion, and affirmation.

But as she continued to explain the difficulty she felt in trusting people to be good to her, it became clear to me that she needed to do more than face the wickedness of her parents and repair the damage they had done to her identity by their brutal treatment.

After we had talked some more about the horrors of her past, I asked her, "This may sound like an odd question, but I wonder, are you able to worship God?"

"No!" she said immediately. "I remember praying to God when I was in that duct, asking him to let me die. I think that was the first time I ever prayed. And he didn't come through for me then. How can I worship a God who wouldn't protect a little girl from that kind of abuse?" She was enraged at God.

Abused by her parents and feeling abandoned by God, she had determined that there was only one person she could rely on—herself.

As a result, in all her relationships, she demanded that others prove themselves worthy of her trust. She expended great energy trying to discern whether people genuinely cared about her. When she found a flaw in their love, which of course she always did, she angrily retreated, just as she had with God.

To her the command to love others was an intolerable burden imposed by an insensitive God, and it made her even more furious if anyone admonished her to be more other-centered. Her commitment to preserve her own self against the harshness of an uncaring world seemed not only necessary but completely legitimate. Her commitment to herself did not strike her as stubborn, arrogant, or wrong. To her it felt thoroughly justified, necessary, and right.

This woman was living a self-centered life.

If she was to be restored to the joy of womanhood, she needed more than understanding and affirmation, more than learning to forgive her wicked parents. She needed forgiveness for her angry commitment to finding herself through her own resources, a commitment that daily involved her in violating the command to love God and others.

The Christian life begins and continues on the foundation of forgiveness, not on a promise of protection and help in a difficult world. Until this woman could define her own self-centeredness as a more serious problem than the hurts and disappointments and wounds that life had brought her, horrible though those were, she would continue to demand help from God but never learn to humbly thank him for his forgiveness.

We do need an approach to relationships that takes seriously our commitment to ourselves, an approach that refuses to justify an attitude of defiant independence of God, an approach that puts us in a place where we recognize the grace of God as our most valued possession.

# *Two*

## Facing Ourselves Honestly

*We are too quick to resent and feel what we suffer from others, but fail to consider how much others suffer from us. Whoever considers his own defects fully and honestly will find no reason to judge others harshly.*

THOMAS À KEMPIS

*Should a counselor encourage troubled partners in a* marriage to explore their own individual hurts to regain a sense of wholeness or is it better to lay out the responsibilities of husbands and wives and to require each to do his or her part?

If you believe that a disappointing and sometimes evil world has damaged people's identity to the point where repair is required before anything else can be done, the first alternative will make sense. If you regard marital problems as nothing more than the result of failure to do what God says, the second option will seem right.

But if you agree that self-centeredness is deeply entrenched in the human soul, that it lingers with surprising and subtle strength even in Christians, then a third approach is needed. Honestly admitting how badly we've been hurt has its place (often an important one), and committing ourselves to obedience is always necessary. But if self-centeredness is stubbornly rooted in our patterns of relating, then exploring our wounds or determining to be good will not be enough.

How can we come to grips with the self-centeredness that is robbing us of joy and our spouses of blessing? What does it take to become people who are growing in an other-centeredness that our mates can taste? Perhaps the first step is to honestly face what is going on within us as we relate to others, to think about what is happening beneath the surface of our relationships.

## THE DIFFICULTY OF GETTING ALONG

How on earth are we supposed to get along with one another? Every person I meet has something about them I don't like. And at some point in our lives we all come to realize that no one cares about us as fully or consistently as we wish he or she would.

Most people, at times, display a mean-spirited pettiness; we are all capable of being thoughtless, abrupt, and demeaning. When we move beyond surface chit-chat, we quickly realize that the person to whom we're talking, whether it be our spouse, parent, child, friend, or pastor, is really more devoted to his or her own well-being than to ours. Some disguise their self-interest behind good listening skills and an almost satisfying warmth. Others parade it without shame.

Occasional flashes of insight, which can rudely arrive at inconvenient times to spoil a good sulk, make us see the same flaws in ourselves. We, like those we criticize, don't care about anyone else more than we care about ourselves. But it doesn't seem as bad in us as it does in them. For us, self-interest simply *is;* we didn't work to develop it. It's as natural as breathing.

What we do and how we feel in our relationships seems so fully understandable to us. We know how insecure and frightened we feel, how badly the wounds we've suffered from mistreatment have damaged our confidence. And we know, too, how hard it can be to function as well as we do. On some mornings, just getting out of bed and brushing our teeth can feel heroic.

For some of us, the morning alarm means another day of fighting overwhelming temptations to binge on food or of living with deviant sexual urges nearly impossible to keep under control. Others of us face more ordinary, but no less exhausting, battles: getting three kids ready for school for the four thousandth time, attending another sales meeting to present a discouraging report, enduring terrible traffic on the way to a job we dislike, and wondering if we'll be able to survive the loneliness that will engulf us when we once more sit down to dinner by ourselves. Most of us are tired—very, very tired. And the future looks gray.

We all live with painful memories and thoughts—some clear, some current, some faded—gone but still strangely felt. We live with humiliating moments like the time when, in front of our friends, Dad said, "When are you going to quit wetting your bed?" We recall doing wrong things that we cannot stop, but joking with friends about others who do the same thing. We suffer recurring nightmares of emotional, physical, and sexual abuse.

But no one knows what battles we are fighting, at least no one knows as we do. To a few trusted friends, we hint at some of our struggles, and maybe, in a moment of courage, share them explicitly with a special friend or counselor. And it feels good to distribute the burden, to observe our friend stay involved with us and not back away. But, no matter how empathic our friends are, none of them feels the same sting in their hearts as we do.

## IF OTHERS ONLY KNEW

We don't often put it this way, but it rings true if we think about it: we believe that if others knew the extent of our pain, they would be less inclined to judge us for our self-concern. No one criticizes a man who disruptively walks out of church in the middle of the sermon once they find out he was suffering a kidney-stone attack.

If people *really* knew, if they could feel all that we've endured and how hard it sometimes is to keep going, then they likely would admire us for the good qualities we somehow have managed to develop in the midst of hardships. Self-interest, especially *our* self-interest, seems understandable. And when we believe that being understood is our deepest need, self-interest seems not merely justified, but entirely normal.

But nobody knows the troubles we've seen, not fully. And so others unfairly criticize us for not being there for them. We always fall short in our efforts to communicate all that is going on inside us; we feel so much more than words can convey, and we quickly realize that no one is listening to us anyhow, not really. We move on, feeling angry, tired, and a bit noble, sitting alone in the silence of misunderstood isolation.

Our one hope is God. He understands; he is with us, cheering our efforts, appreciating how hard things can be. And we feel better, strengthened in our self-admiration by our image of a divine grandfather appreciatively sighing as he watches us carry on. He knows, therefore he is impressed with us. So we think.

Some people never permit themselves to feel this level of aloneness. Pretending that they don't long for richer love, more meaning, and deeper relationships, they manage to feel pretty good most of the time.

Others, a few truly joyful folks, know that what their souls yearn for is coming. They enjoy the good things available now, tolerating with cheerful grace the imperfections. These mature saints speak of a deep longing for what is not yet theirs, a deep longing that sometimes becomes an intense ache of the soul. Honest Christians hurt. Mature honest Christians understand groaning but surround their hurt with the joy of service and anticipation.

Most of us, however, struggle on with false nobility, disguising our rage against God for protecting us so poorly with the idea that he gratefully appreciates our worthy efforts to remain faithful.

## ONE PLACE WHERE WE CAN'T PRETEND

One place, however, where it is nearly impossible to block out the real struggles of getting along with people who don't care about us as we desire, and where false nobility is insufficient comfort, is marriage.

You can get away from friends, sometimes far away. Some "friendships" (I'm using the word loosely) have avoided total disintegration only because of distance. Often, when one friend has relocated, the "relationship" gradually dwindles to a quickly signed Christmas card.

But married couples are denied this option. Living at a distance may be attractive, but as a permanent solution, clearly won't work. Husbands and wives are supposed to live together, sleep together, eat together, spend money together (or at least from a common fund), vacation together, socialize together, raise children together, worship together, face conflict together.

Exactly how are we supposed to do all those things with someone who neither fully understands nor fully cares about us, someone who can be so selfish? How are we supposed to make it enjoyable? Most agree, of course, that a few separate interests and friends, even occasional separate trips, may be healthy, but being together, sharing *life* together, is meant to be the unique joy of marriage.

For some it is; for many it is not. Almost half of all married couples, both in the church and out, eventually experience togetherness as something bad and difficult to endure, something so maddening and painful that separation, immediate and permanent, seems necessary for personal survival, for sanity, for any hope of happiness. (It's worth noticing, in passing, that when we believe personal survival is at stake, questions about the moral rightness of a choice tend to become secondary.)

## SURPRISES AFTER THE CEREMONY

Since no one marries with plans to be miserable, many men and women face rude and shocking surprises after the ceremony. How many women have mistaken broad shoulders for character strength and ended up with a well-built wimp? How many thought that a man's drive for success and a master's degree in business promised an interesting, prosperous life and later discovered that they spelled family neglect, eighty-hour work weeks, and cardiac disease?

I was in Arkansas, speaking to a group of church leaders on biblical counseling. After I had given a lecture on marriage, a well-dressed couple in their early thirties approached me. He, tall and stylishly dressed, carried himself with an air of easy confidence. She, beautiful and wearing a well-tailored Anne Klein suit, smiled nervously, shifting her weight from one foot to the other.

"Dr. Crabb," the husband said, "something you said caught my attention. May we have a few minutes of your time?"

We found a quiet place to sit, and he began, "God has blessed us with two wonderful kids, a good income, and an interesting life. And we're really very close, but I sometimes feel something is missing." He spoke with an untroubled calmness.

As I listened to his words, I felt entirely unengaged. He could have been reading from the phone book and had the same effect.

Because our time was short, I took a risk. I turned to his wife and said, "Let me guess. Right now you'd like to scream, but your husband is so nice and provides so well for you that you assume whatever frustration you feel must be all your fault. If you were honest, you'd tell him how completely untouched you feel by him and how much you sometimes hate his charm and money because he's not giving you the involvement you want."

She burst into tears. "That's exactly how I feel. When I married him, I knew he was on the road to success, and I thought he was the kind of man I wanted. We have everything money can buy, but we have nothing. I'd give it all away if I knew he really *wanted* me. I never thought it would turn out like this."

Men can be equally lacking in the skill of reading people. A friend of mine, headed for the mission field, was attracted to a woman because of her quiet steadiness and Christian piety, qualities he thought reflected a mature strength that would equip her to richly "be there" during good times and bad.

He was wrong. The shyness during honeymoon days soon gave way to active coldness and utter disinterest in physical contact, problems that made no sense till years later when a therapist elicited reports of sexual abuse at the hands of her father, a highly respected leader in Christian circles. What my friend had taken to be spiritual stability, he later came to realize was a fiercely maintained internal deadness that muted intolerable memories.

## THE HONEYMOON ALWAYS ENDS

No marriage is free from tensions. The honeymoon always ends, if not within a few hours, then often within weeks or months. We all marry someone defective and selfish; some are less selfish than others perhaps, but we are all infected with the same disease. Eventually it surfaces, and if untreated, it is fatal to relationships.

Sometimes the honeymoon gives way to stable harmony achieved at the cost of an agreed-upon distance. "You don't bother me about this and I won't bring up that." This sort of arrangement, one that accommodates selfishness through an emotional separation that avoids confrontation, can last for years, culminating in a fiftieth-anniversary celebration where the toast is flat and the kiss forced.

Occasionally the immature bliss of honeymoon love yields to a growing relationship between people who notice their own flaws more than those of their mates, who are troubled more by their own selfishness than by that of their spouse, and who make a priority to become better companions. These become the truly great marriages, and they are rare.

More common are marriages where the partners' flaws are too obvious to be overlooked. Money and fun aren't sufficient to support patient endurance of infidelity, aloofness, nasty jabs, paranoid suspiciousness, refusal to talk things over, impulsive and revenge-motivated spending, sexual coldness, unwillingness to admit error, and religious stuffiness. When a spouse exhibits any of these as a pattern, more than as occasional lapses, it seems impossible for mere mortals to uncomplainingly accept. Something must be done.

One of my clients, I'll call her Susan, described the kind of hurt, anger, and frantic desperation such situations arouse:

I just don't know what to do anymore. I really don't. I never thought I'd hear myself say these words but sometimes I really want to leave him; just get a divorce and get away. He is impossible to live with.

I know divorce is wrong. And besides, I don't have any money. So I'm stuck.

I've tried for years to submit to him, to do whatever he wanted me to do; but all I have to show for my effort is an angry husband who tells me everything I do wrong. And I'm miserable. I'm desperate!

It doesn't do any good to talk to him. He never listens, even when I scream. If I try to be logical, he tells me I'm stupid. If I try to listen to how he feels and do all that I can do to please him (particularly in bed), then he is usually happy with me—for a while. But the minute I do something wrong, I get it again.

I pray a lot—if it weren't for God I'd probably be totally crazy—but I know he doesn't guarantee he'll change my husband—and I'm not sure how he wants me to change. If he wants me to do everything that pleases my husband, I just can't do it. Any suggestions?

Monologues like this make me wish I'd gone into plumbing. Leaky pipes can be fixed or replaced. But what do you do with mean husbands who think their wives are the real problem or angry wives convinced of the reverse, both of whom, in addition to being mean and angry, experience intolerable levels of pain? Do you replace them? It may be tempting, but Christians are supposed to be fixable. So what do you do?

Do you:

- —work to improve communication?
- —confront irresponsibility?
- —encourage continued efforts to do the right thing?
- —come up with specific plans to intervene?
- —relate with the woundedness, frustration, and pain?
- —disentangle co-dependent patterns of relating?
- —speak of freedom to become all that you can be?

Do you recommend counseling, and, if so, what sort? Insight-oriented? Biblical-exhortational? Family systems? Existential?

## TRADITIONALISTS VS. EGALITARIANS

In the previous chapter, I discussed two popular approaches to building relationships: one that stresses self-development as the route to harmony and one that emphasizes our responsibility to conform to a biblical model of marriage.

Among those who agree that the Bible provides authoritative instruction, a serious disagreement has arisen over what a biblical marriage really looks like. *Traditionalists* (a term I use with no intended negative connotation) believe that it is a husband's responsibility to lead as the head of the home and that a wife should faithfully submit to her husband's leadership.

*Egalitarians,* Christians who dispute the traditional

view that male headship involves decision-making authority over the wife, emphasize mutual submission in which each partner submits to the other in a relationship between equals.

Traditionalists define the responsibilities of husbands and wives and then encourage each partner to fulfill his or her role within the marriage. Egalitarians, concerned that women have been unfairly repressed by a male-biased interpretation of headship and submission, encourage women to affirm their equality with men in a relationship between partners rather than to order themselves "under" a man's authority in a hierarchical relationship. The first view, it might be noted, can sometimes run dangerously close to joyless moralism; the second can too easily degenerate into a focus on self-development. I discussed both errors in the previous chapter.

At the moment, I am less concerned with whether the traditional or egalitarian view enjoys clearer biblical support than I am with what I think the Bible regards as a far more important matter, a matter which folks caught up with either fitting into roles or pushing their way out of them may easily overlook.

I fear that neither position, as is often communicated by teachers and understood and practiced by ordinary people trying to get along in their marriages, adequately gets at the real problem destroying relationships. People can live as either traditionalists or egalitarians and never notice—let alone challenge—their strong undercurrents of self-centeredness.

Traditionalists are rightly concerned with biblical instructions to husbands and wives. Egalitarians are rightly concerned with understanding those instructions in a way that does not reduce women to inferior status. Traditionalists emphasize that God has designed authority into the structure of human relationships and that it is not right to guard against the abuse of authority by eliminating it. Egalitarians are sensitive to the history of male domination and are looking for ways to honor our equality as redeemed image bearers.

However, when we focus on *either* our responsibilities to do whatever God says *or* our opportunities to live as equally valuable citizens of God's kingdom, then our counsel to troubled spouses may miss the core problem.

Think back to Susan, the unhappy wife who asked me for help. Let's suppose we sent her to two Christian counselors, one traditional and one egalitarian. How would each advise Susan?

Some biblical counselors, a bit rigidly I think, suggest that all counseling interventions should fall into one of the four categories Paul mentions to Timothy: "All Scripture is . . . useful for *teaching, rebuking, correcting* and *training in righteousness*" (2 Tim. 3:16, italics mine). Although I think this model unfairly limits the use of Scripture in counseling, for ease of presentation, I'll follow it here. Helpers committed both to the Bible and to either of the two ideas about a marriage framework might respond as follows. (Brief statements must, to some inescapable degree, represent a caricature of the view they express, but something important about each view is, I think, reflected in the suggested responses.)

As you read these hypothetical responses from a

traditionalist and an egalitarian, pay special attention to whether the counselor is aware of the problem of self-centered commitment.

## TEACHING

### *From a traditionalist:*

Before I can be of help to you, I think we should review Ephesians 5 and 1 Peter 3 to make sure you're clear on God's instructions to women.

### *From an egalitarian:*

God made you as a unique person and intends that you express all that you are for good purposes. In Christ there is neither male nor female, so all role distinctions are erased.

## REBUKING

### *From a traditionalist:*

It's not hard to see that you're very angry. Although your husband may be a source of real suffering for you, Scripture is clear that you are to get rid of all bitterness, rage, and anger. Let's talk about how you can do that.

### *From an egalitarian:*

I really want to help you see how wrong it is for you to be so demeaned by this man, or anyone else for that matter. It's just not right for you to spend half your life trying to keep him from getting mad at you. Look at all the things you're not doing because he intimidates you.

## CORRECTING

### *From a traditionalist:*

The fact that you've alternated between doing everything he wants and rebellious explosions suggests you have a divided heart. Perhaps it's time to think through what you said confused you, namely, how God wants you to change.

### *From an egalitarian:*

You've really bought into the be-a-doormat model, haven't you? No wonder you're angry. God wants you to be who you are, not who your husband demands you be. Perhaps it's time to explore your potential as a person, a glorious creation and re-creation of God, and to take a few steps toward realizing that potential.

## TRAINING IN RIGHTEOUSNESS

### *From a traditionalist:*

I want you to give this questionnaire to your husband. It invites him to evaluate your performance as a wife on a variety of specific measures important to men. Things like personal grooming, meal preparation, interest in his work, and so on. Wherever he rates you low, we'll make it your homework to improve in those areas. Let me give you several Bible verses to memorize and study before we meet again next week. (The other responses are all hypothetical and represent my guesses about what folks from each point of view might say. This one is drawn fairly closely from a published manual on marriage counseling from a traditionalist perspective.)

*From an egalitarian:*

Scripture frees you to speak the truth in love and to grow up into Christ as an equal heir and fully human, redeemed woman. This suggests that you ought to tell your husband exactly what is in your heart and to then begin doing what you believe is best for your growth, not what your husband decides is best for you. Who knows? He may gain respect for you, but if not, at least you'll gain respect for yourself and be living closer to the ideal of a Christian woman.

Certainly there are folks from each camp who would respond in different ways. But these comments capture something of the distinctive emphases of the two positions. The choice for Susan may appear to be between *suffocating* legalism ("This is what you are to do; now do it") and *self-expressing freedom* ("Becoming who you are is what matters most"). Neither one satisfies my understanding of what our Lord has freed Susan to do.

## THE PROBLEM WITH BOTH VIEWS

Something I find objectionable in both traditionalism and egalitarianism is what many think desirable: both positions give practical advice. "Take this list home to your husband" or "If you really want to go back to school, go." In either case, the distressed woman is given a specific plan to follow.

And people like that. We all do. Whether we are "traditional" or "egalitarian," we like knowing what to do. We want our sermons to end with clear applications: handles for understanding, steps to follow. The cry today is for practical help. But that cry, to the degree that it fails to address self-centeredness, may be wrong.

Sometimes, of course, a desire for specific guidance is not only natural but entirely legitimate. "Which way to the bank?" or "How do I set up a budget?" or "Do I need surgery?" On a different level, the jailer was perfectly correct in pressing Paul for a definite answer to his question, "What must I do to be saved?" And Paul, of course, was right in giving one.

But not all requests for help are proper. Sometimes they mask a desire to gain control of a situation, a desire driven by the depraved energy of self-commitment. It is terrifically important to us fallen people to have resources to draw on in times of crisis: "Tell me something I can do that will make a difference." Often the difference we're after, particularly when we're troubled by an unhappy relationship, is a change either in someone else who is causing us pain or in the way we feel, or both. To put it simply: *We want to be in charge of the way we experience life,* and that's the essence of our commitment to ourselves.

Watching a loved one die can bring us to terms with the truth that we cannot control many things that matter deeply to us. At these points, we become enraged, resigned, or yielded, but we are inevitably confronted with our inability to preserve healthy life in our bodies. But what confronts us with our utter powerlessness to promote and preserve abundant life in our souls? Most times we manage to maintain the illusion that we can choose our personal well-being, and sometimes instructions for living the Christian life tend to encourage the idea that if we simply do what we're told, then life will turn out as we want.

## THE FATAL DISEASE OF SELF-CENTEREDNESS

The Christian life doesn't *begin* until we see that the disease of self-centeredness (and its assumption of self-sufficiency) is fatal to our souls and so advanced that efforts at self-cure are useless. Self-centeredness is as morally wrong for an image bearer as cancer is physically abnormal in the human body.

And the Christian life cannot *develop* without a deepening awareness of what we first recognized at the time of our conversion: self-centeredness still runs deep within us, cannot be overcome with hard work and good intentions, and is both fatal and wrong.

Too many efforts to solve marriage problems begin with the question, "How am I supposed to handle this situation?" Traditionalists answer, "Fit into your role." Egalitarians respond, "Be fully human in serving one another." The issue that the different answers reflect is important and must be thought through to the point of personal conviction. But in the heat of arguing which view is correct, a more important question, and one that should be asked first, is rarely raised.

This question, one that must be asked again and again, each time with stronger force, is "How can I escape judgment for being so self-centered?"

A true awareness of ourselves, in every situation and at any point in our spiritual development, will make us more aware of our need of forgiving grace. But think how infrequently we confess our self-centeredness and how often we request God's help or guidance or comfort. Encouragement and direction seem more necessary than pardon. Is our self-awareness so limited that forgiveness seems more like an historical foundation than a currently needed reality?

It is, of course, entirely right to ask God for such things as comfort and guidance, but only with an attitude of humble, joyful appreciation for his redeeming grace. And this attitude can only grow when we take a long, honest look at ourselves and recognize the self-centeredness beneath both our best efforts to obey and our fondest desire for developing our potential to the fullest.

People who find themselves in painful relationships want practical help. And too often it's given without thinking much about the self-centeredness that with frightening regularity fuels the request.

With selfishness still in control, every effort to improve the relationship will create new problems. Traditional husbands try to lead well but complain that their wives neither submit to their leadership nor support them in their struggles. Traditional wives do their best to accommodate their husbands, but often grow resentful over the insensitivity and condescending harshness they endure.

Egalitarian husbands do what they can to encourage their wives' development but may secretly long for more attention and support from their wives. Egalitarian wives move out boldly into their worlds but later wonder if more initiative is really what will take to fill their still unrelieved emptiness.

Only when the central problem of self-centeredness is faced first and squarely can a *desire* to do right develop; then God's instructions become a delight, rather than a box to squeeze into, or an imposition on our freedom.

Married folks would do well to think *less* about doing what good husbands and wives should do or whether they are properly taking their humanness into account, and *more* about how self-directed so much of their activity really is. Rather than figuring out practical ways to improve our marriages, perhaps we need to realize how badly and how often we need forgiveness.

We live in the day of "twelve-step recovery" programs. Everyone wants specific things to do. We want manageable activity and practical handles to guide us through the confusing times in our lives.

But we will not be able to take the positive steps toward the enjoyment marriage was designed to provide until we first take steps to recognize more clearly the selfishness we so easily excuse.

# *Three*

## The Real Problem

*That day of wrath. That dreadful day,*
*When heaven and earth shall pass away;*
*What power shall be the sinner's stay?*
*How shall he meet that dreadful day?*

SIR WALTER SCOTT

*In six weeks I would be twenty-two years old. In three weeks*
I would be a husband. The first I was prepared for;
the second, well, that's what I was here for.

I was sitting on an old worn-velvet loveseat in the
preacher's living room. Nestled close beside me was
Rachael, my beautiful bride-to-be. It would have
been difficult to slide even a thin book between us.

Across from us, in separate chairs perhaps ten
feet apart, sat the preacher and his wife, both in
their late seventies. She nodded her gray head and
smiled and listened and rocked as her hands worked
a rapid rhythm with yarn and knitting needles. He
was relaxed into an old stuffed recliner, busily jot-
ting notes in a small, well-used black notebook.

As we discussed the details of our wedding ceremony, I found myself watching the old couple, not
as preacher and preacher's wife, but as husband
and wife. Suddenly something struck me. Those

two, sitting in separate chairs with more than three yards between them, conveyed more love with a single meeting of their eyes than my fiancée and I were exchanging with all our snuggling, grinning, and whispered endearments.

I still remember thinking, "How do we get from here to there, from where we are in our eager young love to where they are in their loving maturity?"

Marriage is a stage on which real love—the kind the apostle Paul described as the greatest virtue—can be enacted for the world to see: the kind of love that enables us to endure wrong with patience, to resist evil with conviction, to enjoy the good things with gusto, to give richly of ourselves with humility, and to nourish another's soul with long-suffering.

When all these virtues are present, not only is each marriage partner incomparably blessed, but sometimes a couple of young apprentices about to take their place on this same stage can catch a glimpse of what the marriage relationship *could* be—a glimpse that won't let them settle for anything less.

But wanting is one thing; becoming is quite another.

## WHAT GETS IN THE WAY?

Why are so few on the path to enjoying the kind of love the preacher and his wife could share from ten feet apart?

Most of us want to be more loving and patient, but it feels like we're struggling against a power pulling us in the opposite direction. And, like quicksand, that power usually wins. Something has hold of us that won't let go.

Earlier I suggested that freeing ourselves to express all that we can be sometimes leads not to intimacy, but to arrogant independence. And efforts to do right without understanding how deeply selfishness taints our motives leads not to closeness, but to stiff courtesy.

Neither the egalitarian nor the traditional model for understanding biblical marriage strongly enough exposes self-centeredness as our basic problem. The egalitarian's replacing of a hierarchical arrangement with a relationship of mutual freedom could foster an unhealthy interest in developing and freeing oneself, thereby strengthening self-centeredness. The traditionalist's attention to gender-specific roles could encourage a moralistic obedience that hides self-centered purposes behind good behavior.

We need to cut through the debate about headship and submission to expose clearly the insidious and pervasive commitment to ourselves that violates love. Once self-centeredness is recognized as the real culprit and other-centeredness as the highest ideal, then we can ask whether an other-centered marriage will reflect egalitarian freedom or hierarchical order.

First, though, we must focus on the real problem: self-centeredness. And nothing brings self-centeredness more clearly into focus than anger.

## THE EXPERIENCE OF ANGER

Everyone knows what it's like to be angry with someone. And when we're angry, we're not really concerned with the welfare of the person we're mad at. Anger, at least the kind we're familiar with, is incompatible with love.

But two observations about the experience of anger often escape our notice. First, *we can be angry and not know it*. Parents are sometimes deeply resentful of their children, but they hide their resentment behind displays of excessive warmth and disciplined reasonableness. An unplanned child, for example, can cause a parent to struggle terribly with bitterness; this may give way to guilt over the bitterness that only suppression can handle. Even planned and fully welcome children, when they don't live up to expectations, can provoke disappointment and anger that parents often mask with strong but insincere declarations of "We love you just as you are." Anger can be present but denied.

The second thing about anger we sometimes fail to notice is that, with frightening ease, *we assume that our anger is justified*. Without thinking through, we see our anger as reasonable, natural, warranted by what's happened, and therefore quite acceptable. Even rage that wishes another harm, the kind of anger good Christians rarely admit to, can seem appropriate.

I was counseling Dennis, a top-level executive with a consulting company. Dennis told me how troubled he was by the strain in his marriage. He and his wife, Marcia, rarely showed affection to each other anymore. Much of the time, Marcia seemed angry and sullen. Dennis was eager to do all he could to relieve the tensions.

In an early session Dennis mentioned in passing a recurrent, puzzling dream. In the dream Marcia, who is perfectly healthy in real life, lay dying of cancer. He was kneeling by her bedside, doing everything in his power to provide comfort. But she wouldn't look at him. She continued to stare at the ceiling, unresponsive to his tearful expressions of love. Dennis had dreamed this dream perhaps a dozen times over the past several years.

A number of sessions later Dennis revealed how Marcia was letting both her body and mind go. She had gained thirty pounds since they married, and she smoked cigarettes and talked on the telephone much of the day. It gradually became clear that he, a professionally up-to-date executive and a regular at the health club, saw Marcia as a fat, boring, undisciplined partner with whom he was stuck for the rest of his life. Because he was a Christian and did not believe in divorce, only her death could provide an acceptable exit from his bondage.

But rather than facing his anger at her and the self-centered approach to life that nourished it, Dennis continued believing he was a patient man doing his best under the circumstances. Pretending patience rather than acknowledging anger preserved his favorable estimate of himself. But his dream had betrayed him.

After reflecting on the dream and looking more honestly at himself, he looked up intently one day and abruptly said, "I really hate her." Now he was angry and he knew it.

But his next sentence was not, "Oh, wretched man that I am! How shall I escape judgment for hating my wife, the one woman in all the world I promised to love?" What he did say was this: "She wasn't careless at all when I met her. She was concerned with her appearance, had a really nice figure, and liked to read and talk about interesting things. I really can't figure out what's happened to her."

He seemed no more bothered by his hatred toward his wife than a friend of mine felt about his impatience with a mechanic over a car that wouldn't start. For both men, blaming someone other than themselves seemed the natural thing to do.

## "YOU MAKE ME ANGRY!"

When we admit to feeling angry, we automatically justify it, as did Dennis, by interpreting other people's actions as adequate cause. Dennis felt he had a right to be angry because Marcia had put on weight and put off reading. Explaining anger by locating its root outside of ourselves is as instinctive as gasping for air when an oxygen supply is cut off. Accepting blame suffocates; shifting blame allows easy breathing. So we shift blame naturally, without effort or thought.

Anger is too revealing an emotion to handle by either *denying its extent* or *finding its cause in someone else,* the two natural ways to deal with it. Anger tells us something about ourselves that deserves attention, something that will need to be exposed and changed before we can move along the path to mature love. To see clearly what keeps us from getting along, look more closely at what happens in us when we are angry.

## LOOKING BENEATH OUR ANGER

A quick peek beneath the surface of anger is enough to see that much of the rage we feel when something bad happens to us grows out of self-centeredness. As we noted earlier, when we become angry, we become less concerned with other people's welfare and more protective of our own.

If left to develop, this diminished concern for the people we're angry with can progress to the point where we may actually relish the thought of their being hurt. From there, it isn't a giant step to so twist our understanding of justice that we come to believe something bad *should* befall them.

We may not hope a car hits them or they lose their job (though thoughts like that do sometimes cross our minds), but we often feel strangely satisfied with the suffering they endure because of our selfish treatment of them. After all, it's what they deserve for how they have wronged us.

Alex and Jane came to me for counseling. Jane had had an affair four years earlier. She repented, begged Alex to accept her back, and worked hard at becoming a supportive, responsive wife.

In my first session with them, Jane said, "It seems that the harder I try to satisfy him, the nastier he gets. I can only handle it for so long. When I fall apart, Alex seems content for a while and lets me alone. But when I start feeling pretty good again, the verbal abuse picks up until he gets me in tears. I'm really tired of this cycle."

Alex sat there, unmoved by Jane's distress. When I asked him how he was feeling, he answered, "It's hard to understand why she should be treated well after all she's done."

When we're this angry, when we feel as Alex did toward his wife, we feel like God is on our side. We join God (really *replace* him) in meting out retribution. But even worse, our indignation over the sins of others blinds us to all sense of personal fault. Alex was not seeing how his focus on himself was contributing to his marital problems. In this condition, we deny ourselves the joys of grace and live as natural men and women, incapable of meaningful love.

Most of us, however, don't let things slide to that degree. We deal with anger more quickly and directly. We check its expression, we forgive, and we behave in a civil and sometimes actually kind fashion, often immediately congratulating ourselves for our "good behavior."

Moral efforts such as these may not lessen anger; more often, they merely cover with a blanket of courtesy containing only a few rips through which our anger leaks out in small doses—little doses that divert personal energy toward ourselves and away from others.

Think how commonly this occurs among "good" people. Reflect on the past few weeks. Remember when you felt annoyed with your spouse, perhaps only mildly and momentarily. Notice what you did or said that was intended to cause pain or get even or keep someone safely under control. Remember when you

- reminded your husband during dinner with friends that the pecan pie was not on his cholesterol-lowering diet

- cast your wife a withering glance for the stupid comment she just made in the Bible study
- corrected, with a lightly superior tone, your husband's error in reporting to friends the date of last year's vacation
- heard your wife start a sentence just as you began reading your favorite newspaper column, consciously tuned her out and then, a few moments later, irritably asked, "What did you say?"
- sat still when you heard the garage door open, knowing that your wife was arriving home with a carful of groceries, then got up only when she stumbled through the door with two overflowing bags and angrily called out, "Are you going to just sit there? I've got six more bags in the trunk."

During each of these interactions, devotion to the partner's happiness was edged out in favor of stronger concern for oneself. In each case, self-centered energy was flowing, fueling anger and directing its expression.

And the anger, as we've already seen, is hard to admit but easy to excuse. Why is something that gets in the way of loving our mate so difficult to recognize? And, more important, why does our anger, and the selfish, hurtful things we do when we're angry, so often seem reasonable and so rarely make us feel truly guilty?

Resentful thoughts should provoke guilt, but more often we regard our bitterness, not as the product of a flaw within us, but as the interplay between our delicate sensitivities and other people's failures. We think others should be rebuked while our damaged souls receive healing. Why is it so hard to see that self-interest, even when offended, is wrong, so wrong that, in fact, we deserve not kindly treatment but the harshest possible judgment?

Some would argue that there's nothing to feel guilty about, at least not when we get angry and stand up for ourselves. When a wife admits to an affair, as Jane did, her husband understandably feels hurt and angry. In most cases, during the period of reconciliation, he needs to tell her honestly how he feels. And a concern to avoid further hurt is completely normal. But when Alex's attitude reflects *no higher priority* than expressing himself and recovering from the blow, then perhaps he is wrongly self-centered.

Others suggest that our anger is really holy anger against sin, the same kind God feels. Maybe we really are right in getting angry with our spouse: "She never supports me when I discipline the kids." "I hate going shopping with him. He always turns his head to look at pretty women." Maybe we are legitimately angry because our spouse is clearly wrong.

But that answer won't do. Calling our anger righteous is a high claim. God's anger never violates his perfect character of holiness and love. In his anger he never perverts justice; he never takes sadistic pleasure in seeing someone suffer, even when it is deserved; and he never compromises or reduces his commitment to people's well-being.

The anger we're more familiar with, the natural and bad kind, points up a fault in our characters that simply isn't there in God's, a fault that interferes with our getting along with one another.

## THE BASIC FLAW

Anger isn't the core issue; nor is the pretense that it doesn't exist. The diminished concern for others that always accompanies anger moves us closer to the central flaw, but doesn't get us quite all the way. And it's not adequate to describe the basic flaw in our character merely as self-centeredness. Certainly this comes close.

Careful inspection of ourselves, particularly when we're angry, makes clear that we suffer from a defect more severe than mere self-centeredness. The greatest obstacle to building truly good relationships is *justified* self-centeredness, a selfishness that, deep in our souls, feels entirely reasonable and therefore acceptable in light of how we've been treated.

The apostle Paul, I think, held a similar notion. Before moving into a clear presentation of the gospel of Christ in his letter to the Romans, Paul spends nearly three chapters clearing away all excuses for sin. When every mouth is stopped and people are utterly unable to justify their sinful, selfish ways before God, *then* Paul introduces the wonder of God's grace. The gospel cannot be enjoyed until all excuses for sin are removed. And the fruit of the gospel—getting along with God and with one another—will develop to the degree that we recognize self-centeredness, see it as inexcusably wrong, and repent of it.

We do, however, have a hard time seeing ourselves as all that guilty. When we confess our faults to God or to one another, we usually try to *explain away* our sin. "You're right. I shouldn't have done that. I was wrong. I'll do my best to not do that again. If only my wife were more supportive, I think I'd have a better chance of licking this problem."

Explanations are requests not for *forgiveness*, but for *understanding*. When we regard our wrong actions as understandable, we feel only a little guilty. But meaningful repentance and enduring change require more than casual confession of guilt. And they also require more than others strongly denouncing our selfishness and firmly exhorting us to selflessness. Movement from self-centeredness toward other-centeredness happens only when we expose our excuses for selfishness and regard those excuses as entirely illegitimate.

But this is not easily done. Whether our sins are big evils, like adultery, spouse-beating, and alcoholism, or lesser ones like impatience, overeating, and gossip, the inclination to excuse ourselves, to see ourselves as right, is terribly strong.

A friend of mine confessed to me that he had committed adultery. He later told me his wife was so unsupportive of the tensions he lived with every day, that his desire to be appreciated by a woman simply got the best of him. "And," he added, "when I explain all of that to my wife, she just doesn't understand. I've decided to do the right thing and stick with my wife, but let me tell you it's hard. It would sure help if she understood me better."

Adulterers often have a distorted perspective on how life works. They see their sin as necessary to their soul's well-being, and therefore more understandable than wrong. And a powerful urge more basic than lust—the wish to be understood and appreciated by a member of the opposite sex—carries them along a path that seems inevitable.

Whatever voice of conscience remains gets swept away like a stick in a tidal wave.

Those of us not guilty of the more heinous sins shake our heads in disbelief that anyone could ever rationalize such obvious evil. We are proudly unaware that the same mechanism for excusing sin operates regularly within us, rendering us vulnerable to the worst sins imaginable.

A simple illustration will make this point clear. A husband arrives home an hour late, detained at the office by pressing deadlines. As he walks through the door, his wife, without bothering to get up from the couch, greets him flatly: "Your meal is on a plate in the micro. You can heat it up if you want."

Immediately he feels defensive, considers explaining his late arrival, then thinks better of it ("What's the use—she's too irritated to listen"). Without saying a word, he walks past her to the bedroom. As he takes off his tie and splashes his face with water, he rehearses an attack on her for her unsupportive attitude, decides to skip it ("It would only cause more hassle"), and just go eat.

It doesn't occur to him that *she* may be feeling neglected and insensitively treated. If it had, the thought of gently moving toward her would feel too risky and weak, certainly uncalled-for at that moment.

He therefore returns to the kitchen, pushes the appropriate buttons on the microwave oven, and stares at his meal through the glass door until the bell sounds. As he carries his plate to the now deserted dinner table, he feels angry satisfaction in meeting her irritability with his noiseless sulk. "Does she really think I *enjoy* working late?" he mutters to himself.

As he plunges his knife into the barely warm meal, his mind drifts to last weekend's shopping trip when *she* bought a dress and *he* passed up the sport coat he had been wanting for months.

As he continues eating, the pleasure generated by his angry thoughts fades; loneliness arrives in its place. He realizes that he could have called to say he would be home later than expected. He decides to make things right with his wife.

He walks to the living room, sits down next to her, and speaking loudly enough to be heard over the television, apologizes for being late. He gently explains his lateness, showing an understanding of his wife's mood.

She softens under the influence of his tender spirit and, with mutual promises to be more thoughtful of one another, they unite in a hug that begins a pleasant evening.

The harmony thereby restored is not solid. The promises are not strong. As I have described this event, it's clear that the husband apologized to relieve his own loneliness rather than to soothe his wife's hurt. Like most apologies, his included an explanation for the offense, making it into a request for understanding. His was not a true apology.

*True apologies never explain*, they only admit, acknowledging that the error was without justifiable cause. Repentant people realize that inexcusable wrong can either be judged or forgiven, never understood and overlooked, and so they beg for forgiveness with no thought of deserving it. Truly repentant people are the ones who begin to grasp God's amazing grace, the ones who know that they need only confess to experience the forgiveness that is always there in infinite supply.

Whether we are adulterers or thoughtless spouses, the problem with all of us is that we stubbornly regard our interpersonal failures not as *inexcusably selfish choices*, but as *understandable mistakes*. The things our spouses do to us seem more like the former; the things we do to them more like the latter.

Excuse-making has been a natural tendency in people ever since Adam blamed Eve and Eve blamed the snake. Without some means of self-justification, we would be forced to face ourselves squarely as we really are, corrupt by God's standards and deserving punishment.

And seeing ourselves as we are would mean taking our place as condemned sinners, worthy of judgment, powerless to improve ourselves, humbled that our very best deeds provide no defense, and utterly at the mercy of a righteously angry Judge. This doesn't sound like much fun. Surely the path to the top would never begin with a descent *this* steep! How can joy emerge from such misery?

Perhaps the hardest thing to get through our brain-damaged heads (when Adam fell, he must have fallen on his head) is that this painful point of nakedness and humility is not only where life begins, but also where joyful growth continues.

*More than anything else, what gets in the way of getting along is self-centeredness that seems reasonable.* God does his deepest work in making us more truly loving when we more clearly see how utterly ugly our selfishness is.

Getting along with each other requires that we

stop making excuses for all the selfish things we do. And if our tendency toward self-justification can be weakened, perhaps then we will more easily recognize our anger when it's there, call it wrong, and experience the thrill of Christ's forgiveness and the power of his cleansing. We're not condemned and we're empowered to love.

Weakening this inclination to self-justification is hard work. Not many undertake it. Why are we so rarely gripped by our own unworthiness? Why don't we weep in stunned appreciation at the Lord's table? How exactly do we manage to excuse in us what God condemns and then forgives? Perhaps answering this last question will make clear the deep work that real growth in other-centeredness requires.

# *Four*

## Surely I'm Not That Bad!

*Natural men have no higher principle in their hearts than self-love. And herein they do not excel the devils. The devils love themselves and love their own happiness and are afraid of their own misery. And the devils would be as religious as the best of natural man if they were in the same circumstances.*

JONATHAN EDWARDS

*Whatever may be the distinction between men and* women, it is clear that both sexes share one fundamental similarity—they're both fallen. Although the process by which Adam and Eve fell is not identical, both fell, and both men and women are flawed by an inbred disposition to rebel against God and to find life on their own. By turning away from God and depending on their own resources, men and women have made it their first priority to look after their own welfare. Both have become self-centered.

In learning to get along, it is important first to understand this common *moral* identity before sorting out whatever may be our unique *sexual* identities. Once we see how self-centeredness operates to keep us from getting along and then figure out how to become more other-centered, it will then be important to ask whether *masculine* other-centeredness is different from *feminine* other-centeredness. But that's a later topic.

## WHY WE EXCUSE OUR BIGGEST FAULT

At this point in the discussion, I am wondering why self-centeredness, even when we recognize in ourselves, does not seem to be a terribly serious problem.

Many Christians, of course, don't even recognize self-centeredness, particularly those who regard an "inside look" at motives as a concession to the false wisdom of psychology. They have no framework for understanding the subtle operation of self-centeredness. As a result, although their zeal in defending God's Word and promoting righteous living may represent a pursuit of power more than a pursuit of God, they may not ever realize the unloving motivation that lurks beneath their outwardly biblical activity.

Why do friends and spouses, when they do recognize their self-centeredness, spend more energy worrying about their personal aches and pains than repenting of this most basic sin? We casually excuse our biggest fault and, as a result, never progress very far in correcting it.

Some time ago, I took a friend into my confidence and told him of a problem that made me feel ashamed. I confessed to occasional bouts of irrational jealousy when another friend enjoyed applause that normally comes my way.

It had taken some time to work up the courage to share my struggle with my friend, and when I did, I expected him to be thoughtfully intrigued and to explore my problem with compassionate fascination. Instead, his brow furrowed in immediate concern as he replied, "Larry, jealousy is really ugly. I've seen it do terrible things to people." That was it. No follow-up, no question. He changed the subject.

His remark caught me off guard. It was not at all what I had anticipated or wanted. I felt unfairly rebuked, entirely unhelped, and more than a little annoyed. A better counselor, I told myself, would have helped me *understand* my jealousy so that I could better deal with it, not quickly judge me for it.

I now believe that his simple comment, one that broke most of the rules of accepted counseling procedure, had more potential to stimulate deep change than hours of insightful, nonjudgmental exploration ever could have. On the other hand, had I merely accepted his comment as a scolding, confessed my jealousy as sinful, and tried hard to act in ways that did not reflect a jealous attitude, change would have been quickly aborted. In other words, had I heard his rebuke as an exhortation to moralistic living, I would not have been helped. Neither insight nor exhortation, by themselves, will ever change us from self-centered to other-centered people.

## TWO WAYS OF DEALING WITH SIN

When we realize we've done something wrong, we typically do one of two things: *either* we quickly apologize *or* we wonder why we did it. The first response looks biblical but often reflects a shallow repentance that leads to no enduring change. The second keeps counselors in business but, like the first one, rarely leads to joyful other-centeredness.

The common temptation to resolve things quickly might have encouraged me to adopt the first method in response to my friend's rebuke: "Lord, I admit I'm jealous. Yes, I know it is wrong. Please forgive and cleanse me."

After I confess, this common approach to Christian living exhorts me to believe that I've been forgiven on the authority of 1 John 1:9* and to behave accordingly. But quick apologies often aren't confessions at all; rather they may hide a determination not to face how deeply sinful we are. The result is a lingering sense of guilt, fear, and resentment: "Something's still very wrong; what would happen if I faced how bad I really am; why does God make it so hard to please him?"

Honest Christians are disturbed when they notice that their version of confession does not reliably lead to the *joys of forgiveness* and the *release of cleansing*. But rather than inviting God's Spirit to impress upon them how badly they need grace, too many sincere believers assume that insight into their problem is the key, that understanding why they sin will give them victory.

This is the second way we deal with sin. Modern psychology encourages us to see internal damage

---

*"If we confess our sins, he is faithful and just and will forgive us our sins and purify us from all unrighteousness."

to our identity as a more serious problem than commitment to self. Notice clearly how our thinking shifts when *understanding the reasons for sin* replaces *repenting of sin*: We view *the wound in our souls as responsible for problems like jealousy, making pain a more basic concern than sin.*

Think how naturally we explain *our* impatience with the kids as the product of a frustrating day at work and how easily we regard *their* impatience as an expression of selfishness worthy of discipline. What an incredible double standard!

In this way of thinking, victory over sin requires that our damaged psyches be healed. No longer is jealousy the fundamental concern. Jealousy becomes the symptom of a wounded, hurting soul, and therapy, complete with understanding, insight, and compassion, becomes the cure. *Forgiveness rooted in grace* may still be seen as necessary for the symptom, but *therapy built on insight* is regarded as essential in treating the more serious problem of internal damage. We shift away from defining the problem as sin (which, in its moralistic form, shouts, "You're jealous. That's sin. Repent!") to seeing it as emotional damage ("Beneath your jealousy is deep hurt that needs healing.").

## THE TWO WAYS ARE NOT SO DIFFERENT

Is this second way of dealing with sin really a shift from the way moralists often think? Is it not true that when we confess our sins, and, perhaps in the letter rather than the spirit of 1 John 1:9, seek forgiveness and expect cleansing, we may feel the *ugliness* of jealousy less than its *embarrassment* and *inconvenience?*

If we stay away from counseling and remain

faithful to a more "spiritual" approach, don't many of us still manage to slip a word of explanation into our confession? And don't most of us cling to the notion that we would not be so jealous were it not for our deep sensitivities as emotionally scarred people and for the insensitivities of others, who seem to us more sinful than scarred?

A moralistic approach that defines sin as merely wrong behavior fails to get at the root problem of justified self-centeredness any better than a more psychological approach that stresses damage as central. Whenever people proudly acknowledge that their problem is sin, you can be certain they have no idea what they are talking about. And when confession is easily made, followed by confident resolve to bear the fruit of repentance, you can conclude the same thing. Unless Christian teachers bear the marks of brokenness, their teaching will not highlight grace. More often, their study of Scripture will feed a harsh judgmentalism that enforces rules and delights to reprimand. Such teaching will entice few to follow Christ.

There is no such thing as "easy" confession. True confession is always an agonizing process. Brokenness over personal sin is a necessary step in learning to love graciously. Routine confession of easily admitted sin does not deal adequately with our faults. *Neither a surface look at sin nor a deep look at damage will disrupt self-centeredness.*

## A THIRD WAY

So what should one do to disrupt self-centeredness? When my friend states that my jealousy is ugly, I should ask myself first whether I agree with his evaluation. If I do, then I need to ask whether I am gripped by the ugliness of my attitude to the point of brokenness. Am I reduced to begging for mercy, and then enjoying its limitless availability?

For most of us, the honest answer to this question will be no. We rarely feel deeply broken by our sinfulness. When we admit that we are not broken, we must then notice how strongly we resist seeing our jealousy (or impatience or pettiness) as truly ugly. We prefer to view ourselves as fascinating, complex, and deep, and to see our ugliness as an unfortunate *by-product* of our complexity.

But, if my friend's response was wise, and I believe it was, then I must ask why his words bothered me. Why is it so difficult to realize that my personal ugliness is a more basic problem than my confusing complexity? Why does insight into my make-up seem more helpful to growth than conviction over my selfishness? Why do I so strongly resist the biblical idea that the root of all my problems is not my *personal identity* as an underdeveloped self, but my *moral identity* as a selfish person still driven, in deep ways, by selfish energy.

Whether we are moralists who deal with every personal problem by confessing sin, or enlightened moderns who search our souls to recover some measure of wholeness in a damaging world, we each tend to think that our needs and longings need more immediate attention than our self-centeredness.

Self-centeredness convincingly and continually whispers to me that nothing in this universe is more important than my need to be accepted and respectfully treated. Nothing is more necessary to understand than my neediness, in all its complexity and depth. If people were really moral, murmurs self, then everyone who crosses my path, whether shopkeeper, pastor, or spouse, would devote their resources to making me whole, happy, and comfortable. If I am in a hurry, you should yield your place in line. If I patiently wait, I am worthy of applause. What I want should determine your response to me. This is the final ethic of self-centeredness.

But it is entirely wrong. Desires related to my humanness (I like people to treat me kindly and fairly) have a place, but not first place. Just as I must open a door before entering a room, so I must deal with the ugliness of my self-centered way of living before I can properly handle my humanness.

We really don't see our self-centeredness as ugly, and therefore we work on other concerns. It seems more important either to live out our potential or to do right things than to face our ugliness. Why? Why do we dismiss our self-centeredness either as a problem easily handled by shallow confession and moral discipline or as something caused by a more basic wound that needs not forgiveness, but therapeutic healing?

The answer, I think, comes in two parts. First, we experience life as isolating and damaging, and second, we see God as an unhurried judge.

## LIFE IS ISOLATING AND DAMAGING

Think back to the woman who, as a little girl, was sold for rent and stuffed in a heating duct for three days. It would be wickedly insensitive to simply tell her she is self-centered and needs to repent. She was hurting, and her hurt was legitimate.

If a counselor could listen to this woman without feeling deeply moved by her pain, if his or her eyes didn't moisten and heart didn't sink a thousand feet, then this counselor should refuse to offer counsel as firmly as I refuse to perform brain surgery. This counselor isn't qualified to represent the heart of God.

The key to providing biblical help is to feel another's pain deeply while still regarding God's forgiveness for sin as the foundation of all helping efforts. Let me explain.

Since the fall, each of us, in a very real sense, lives alone. No one else is able to climb inside our skin. We feel our hurts with a sharpness that no one else experiences, no matter how empathetically they weep with us.

People care, but they cannot meet our needs. Many times, professions of interest from others seem hollow. Loyalty is rare, affection is fickle, and we feel isolated, even in the midst of communities designed to care.

We long to be touched, to feel someone else's presence. But the strange, sad truth is that this loneliness is most commonly relieved through mistreatment. We feel the pain of someone's unkindness more deeply than the joy of another's compassion. In a fallen world, the most profoundly experienced human touch is often one that hurts. Well-intentioned friends manage to speak exactly the wrong words when we most need to hear the right ones, and the keenly felt sting can last for years. Loving spouses occasionally reveal a meanness that warns us never to take their kindness for granted. Keep your guard up; you can never be quite sure what might trigger the feared anger. Never go off duty; you might be destroyed.

For some, the wounds from mistreatment are deep, and pervasively affect their functioning. Grim stories of physical and sexual abuse are surfacing more and more in modern culture, reminding us that the pain of some goes far beyond the hurt that mere rudeness can generate.*

Other folks feel neither lonely nor mistreated, but their reported contentment does not always indicate maturity. Carefree happiness often characterizes people caught up in self-indulgent living, people who refuse to face matters of deep morality. "I'll always be happy and never have trouble," says the wicked in Psalm 10:6.

Generally, people who experience no painful loneliness are blissfully unaware of the wonderful intimacies they were designed to enjoy. They win contentment by asking less of life and pretending that they want no more than they have. If they are Christians, they may bury personal pain beneath the strong pleasure of indulging whatever urges they can respectably satisfy, perhaps more Christian activity to gain approval, or in-depth Bible study to learn what can then be paraded.

But handling life this way is an insult to the One who is now preparing a far better place for us. Spiritual growth includes an awakening of deep longings within us that make us eagerly anticipate heaven. This awakening leads to the

---

*For an excellent discussion of the difficult topic of sexual abuse, see *The Wounded Heart* by Dan Allender. Dr. Allender realistically faces the extent of damage but still insists that repentance from self-centeredness is central in the process of recovery.

true contentment of asking less of this life because more is coming in the next, but also deepens our loneliness and sense of mistreatment here on earth.

Most of us admit that life is rough. Things do not always go as we want, and we hurt. Illness, financial reverses, betrayal by a friend, an uncaring spouse—life simply is not easy. Continuing on with everyday responsibilities can sometimes feel like climbing a steep hill with a heavy weight strapped to our back.

And then we're inclined to reason like this: "If anyone knew how difficult my life has been, how lonely and wounded I feel, and if anyone knew how hard it has been for me to do as well as I have, surely I would not be asked to do more. I am so hurt and so weary that it's time someone came through for me. Anyone who really knew everything I've been through would take care of me."

Although this attitude may be imbedded within our way of thinking, it often lies dormant until a particularly trying day comes along. As long as things continue on reasonably well, most of us manage to live decently responsible and caring lives. But when we are shaken, when circumstances remind us of our aloneness, and people treat us unkindly, then we hibernate, feeling that we no longer have to be other-centered.

Wives have a special knack for requesting help with a project at the moment when husbands are most enjoying a few moments of rest. Husbands tend to feel sexually aroused at times when wives are least willing to tumble into bed. And the thought mechanism engages: "If my husband/wife really knew how I feel right now and all that I've been through today, then he/she would realize that it is just not right to require anything of me. The way I'm being treated just proves his/her insensitivity. What I ought to get is an offer of a cup of coffee or a back rub." The struggles we endure and the loneliness we feel justify our self-centered focus.

It's more than interesting to notice how unblemished humanity responds to aloneness and mistreatment. As our Lord hung on the cross, he didn't require others to treat him fairly. Even though he was alone and wrongly treated beyond imagination and even though he mightily wished his pain could be avoided, his commitment to the Father's purpose and to rescuing us from judgment never became secondary to his desire for immediate relief. It would never have occurred to him to use suffering to excuse self-interest.

When *we* hurt, however, we *do* use our suffering to excuse our self-interest. Self-centeredness seems understandable. A command to think of another's happiness seems cruel and absurd. When our Lord hurt, other-centeredness came naturally: "Father, forgive them, for they do not know what they are doing." In us, loneliness and abuse justify whatever effort we make to recover our sense of dignity and worth, to preserve our meager quality of life. In Christ, however, loneliness and abuse provided a backdrop for highlighting the difference between a character that justifies self-interest and one that delights to love: "Today you will be with me in paradise."

Living for our own interests simply does not seem wrong when we feel alone and wounded. Our struggles in life can make self-centeredness appear not only reasonable, but also right. "If only people knew how empty and hurt I really feel . . ."

An isolating and damaging world makes it seem reasonable to look out for oneself. But another factor, perhaps a stronger one, further encourages us to excuse and justify self-centeredness.

## GOD IS AN UNHURRIED JUDGE

As a boy, I was careful to not commit an obvious sin the day before exams. Although I was taught better, I thought of God as an old, perhaps a little mean-spirited neighbor, the sort who made you tremble if ever a ball flew accidentally into his yard. If I sinned, I was quite certain that retribution would be swift and severe.

But occasionally I would slip up and do something I thought terrible on a Tuesday night, and then score a high grade on Wednesday's exam. I remember feeling confused. Did it really not matter that I had done wrong? Could balls routinely land in the neighbor's yard without consequence? Maybe kids running through his flower garden to retrieve their ball didn't really bother the old man. Was God indifferent to whether I behaved well or lapsed into serious sin?

Think for a moment of the thousands of times we all have felt the stab of conscience after doing something wrong: "Uh oh! That was wrong. I'm in for it now." Then nothing happened.

Or, the other way around. How often have we resisted a favorite temptation, and then stood in line to receive divine favor, only to run headlong into trouble: a "D" on the exam, a flat tire, a bad medical report, or our husband's affair.

Living in this world, the way God runs it, makes it likely that we'll catch the germ of fatalism: whatever will be, will be. Some of us come down with a bad case of it, believing that it makes little difference whether we're good or bad.

We do our best to train our children properly and our seventeen-year-old daughter gets pregnant. We pray for God's leading in the choice of a mate and find out five years after the wedding that our husband is actively homosexual. We provide well for our families and never watch pornographic movies in our hotel rooms during business trips, and our wife has an affair with a colleague. We do everything we can to please our mates and still, after twenty-eight years, our husband grumbles when his coffee isn't hot.

Does good living pay? Or does bad living pay equally well, maybe better? Perhaps we have kept our hearts pure and washed our hands in vain (Ps. 73:13).

In Peter's day, some were asking, "Where is this 'coming' he promised . . . Everything goes on as it has since the beginning of creation" (2 Peter 3:4). Like those first-century Christians, we look around us, in restaurants, at movie advertisements, and in business, and notice that "the wicked freely strut about when what is vile is honored among men" (Ps. 12:8).

Perhaps "God has forgotten; he covers his face and never sees" (Ps. 10:11). Is God like the parents who don't want to know that their child is abusing drugs and therefore close their eyes to all the evidence? Children in this kind of home learn quickly that they are free to do whatever they want without consequence. Apparently the bad things we're told never to do aren't so bad after all.

The thing we notice is this: in spite of thunderous warnings delivered from well-pounded pulpits, our self-centeredness seems to generate few bad consequences. And every youngster knows that shouting can be easily endured if there are no spankings.

God seems in no hurry to judge. For now, it appears we can live self-centeredly and not pay a price.

But we can interpret God's delay in *two* ways: either our sin doesn't really offend him a great deal or " . . . he is patient with [us], not wanting anyone to perish, but everyone to come to repentance" (2 Peter 3:9).

In our fallen way of thinking, we strongly favor explaining withheld judgment in terms of divine indifference. If God, the ultimate standard of morality who has the power to punish and reward, is not all that bothered by our self-centered ways, then we can carry on with whatever makes us feel good without worrying about punishment for wrongdoing and without giving up our good opinion of ourselves.

Our conscience can be happily ignored. Unpleasant twinges of guilt can be written off as neurotic leftovers from a childhood full of imagined fears that maturity outgrows, fears of bogeymen in closets and alligators under beds.

And so we are inclined to regard ordinary self-centeredness as a rather insignificant problem. Most of us denounce infidelity and tax evasion as wrong but remain comfortably inattentive to our habit of talking about ourselves more than asking questions of others or letting our spouse always clean up the mess in the bathroom. The examples are legion.

The truth is we can continue on with our everyday failings, at least for a time, without being struck by lightning. And the unpleasant things that happen seem evenly distributed between good people and bad people.

And when we look after ourselves, better things often do come our way. God's unhurried ways can encourage us to think casually about our ongoing struggle with sin.

Two elements then contribute to our casual attitude toward sin: (1) an isolating and damaging world that provides us with excuses for self-centeredness and (2) God's delayed judgment, which we misinterpret to mean that he isn't all that bothered by our sin. As a result, we value a richer understanding of ourselves more than a deeper conviction of sin.

Having dismissed our selfishness as a relatively benign disorder, we are free to keep our focus on what really matters to self-centered people: the immediate quality of our lives. Finding a way to heal our wounds and to restore a sense of personal wholeness continues to be a far more pressing concern than knowing the escape route from judgment and worshiping the one who provided it.

And the disease continues unchecked, ruining relationships and carrying us toward certain judgment.

# *Five*

## Change is Possible

*The beginning of repentance is a sense of God's mercy.*
JOHN CALVIN

"Okay, I'm selfish. So what else is new." We tend to view self-centeredness the way we look at eating a second dessert: it may not be right, but it isn't that big a problem. Most of us are occupied with other, much more serious problems—controlling our sexual appetites, coping with loneliness, trying to get along with family and colleagues, making financial ends meet, keeping ourselves in decent health. Selfishness just doesn't feel like a major concern. But it is!

Unless we are struck with the inexcusable wrongness and the deadly power of self-centeredness, we will not make much progress in becoming other-centered. We will overlook the selfish motives rumbling beneath much of what we do, and we will dismiss as acceptable error whatever selfishness we do own: "Well, yes, it is terribly wrong to think only of oneself. We mustn't do that."

Times when we are struck with the sheer evil of self-centeredness cannot be arranged. Most often, they come at surprising times and deliver unexpected impact. One of those moments seized me during a casual conversation.

I was sitting in an outdoor cafe in Capetown, enjoying coffee and conversation with British theologian D. Broughton Knox. Around us bustled the life of the beautiful South African city. Rising behind us was the awesome backdrop of cold mountains, shooting up proudly and then disappearing indifferently into white clouds. To one side, open fields stretched for acres, blooming with nature's patchwork quilt of wildflowers.

A comfortable pause in our conversation allowed the surrounding beauty to put me in a pensive mood. Finally I broke the silence by posing to my companion what I thought was a complex and thoughtful question, the kind that lesser minds wrangle over for generations.

"Why is it, do you suppose, that people have such a hard time getting along with each other?"

Dr. Knox is well known for his brilliant mind and is even seen by some as rather formidable. Challenging his views is risky business, for he never adopts a position without carefully thinking through the alternatives. He's also able to express important ideas in simple words because he understands those ideas so well.

As I spoke he watched me with flattering attention. Then, with neither arrogance nor hesitation, he said, "Well, the whole thing comes down to selfishness, doesn't it. Isn't it interesting how people complicate it all so much? I suppose we don't like seeing ourselves as we really are."

The fresh clarity and strong impact of his words staggered me. What enormous implications they held: All our relationship problems spring from one place—the foul well of selfishness!

If this is true, I thought, then the real problem we must tackle is to understand how self-centered people can become other-centered people.

Since then, however, I have realized that we must work on another problem first. It rarely has impact to be told that we are really selfish. Many of us readily plead guilty to the charge. Privately, of course, we think the crime is not terribly serious. A misdemeanor perhaps, worthy of a small fine.

Our first job, then, is to attack head-on this reliable habit of thinking that our selfishness is understandable in light of the struggles we face and that more serious concerns require our attention. We must see that fitting into prescribed roles or freeing ourselves from oppression are not the most important things we can do to learn to get along with one another as God intended. These are lower priorities than repenting of self-centeredness.

Every effort we make to restore people to godly functioning must deal with the problem of justified selfishness. Efforts that focus on something else— whether bludgeoning people into conformity through confrontation, or liberating them psychologically through therapy and socially through asserting rights—badly miss the point.

Personal diagnosis is always unpleasant for sinful people. Honest self-evaluation reliably leads to unflattering observations about ourselves. But diagnosis, no matter how deflating, must precede treatment, because it informs us what treatment is needed and makes us gratefully willing to receive it.

What will it take to convince us that our selfishness is without excuse and that our first job, in our friendships and marriages, is to recognize our selfishness and learn how we can change?

To answer this question, we need to grasp three things: our greatest need is forgiveness, only God's law has the power to shatter our excuses, and change occurs only in the context of hope.

## OUR GREATEST NEED IS FORGIVENESS

In John Bunyan's classic allegory, *Pilgrim's Progress*, Pilgrim, the main character, begins his journey weighted down by a heavy burden strapped tightly to his back. Like a severe toothache, this load fully consumes his attention. Nothing matters more to him than getting free of it.

The intolerable weight represents Pilgrim's sin, and he cannot gain relief from it until, after climbing a hill, he finds forgiveness waiting for him at the cross. Pilgrim then becomes Christian and sets off in single-minded pursuit of the Celestial City.

If we were to rewrite *Pilgrim's Progress* today, reflecting values prevailing in many of our Christian communities, Pilgrim might be renamed Victim and his burden, rather than sin symbolized by a back-breaking weight, might become a tightly bound soul gasping for air. Or perhaps the burden would be an injured soul, represented by an open wound on his body, inflicted by friends who, with neither cause nor warning, turned on him and used him cruelly for their own advantage.

If the writer of this updated version were a moralist, release from Victim's confinement and recovery from his wound would no doubt come through stern admonishments to obey God, duly heeded by a chastened Victim who, after enough time had elapsed to demonstrate a consistent pattern of moral living, would be called Pharisee.

But poor sales, especially among the growing ranks of free thinkers who despise the restrictions of an authority outside themselves, might quickly lead to a second edition, this one written by someone who understands the thoroughly human cry for freedom.

In this even more updated version (and this one likely would break all sales records), Victim becomes Himself or Herself (or, to avoid any hint of sexism, Itself) and learns to break free from all dependency in relationships and to live a self-affirmed, creatively alive, independent existence. The story ends when Himself or Herself reaches the Kingdom of Self, and lives in utopian harmony with other selves, each one committed entirely to his or her own freedom.*

---

*Observing the long-term effects of living by this philosophy might eventually compel an honest publisher to retitle the work *Victim's Descent into Hell*. I suggest reading the episode in *Pilgrim's Progress* where Pilgrim meets Mr. Worldly Wiseman, who directs him to the town of Morality and to Mr. Legalist and his son Civility. A careful reading of this passage and of Evangelist's rebuke of Pilgrim for heeding Mr. Worldly Wiseman's counsel would be time well spent.

In each new edition, the difficulty is less with the proposed solution and more with the diagnosed problem. Each author has shifted from identifying the burden as *sin* to seeing it as *restriction* or as a personal *wound*.

The moralistic author whose hero became Pharisee would quickly insist with pharisaical indignation that he has not, of course, made that shift. The problem, in his eyes, continues to be sin that must be confronted and abandoned.

But to the degree that his exhortations to holy living are a response to Victim's cry for understanding and help, the moralist has shifted away from a biblical view of sin. Victim's cry for help needs to be heard. He is wounded, injured by the mistreatment of others. His pain needs to be understood, not dismissed with a scolding. *But the use made of this pain—justifying self-centered living— must be exposed and condemned.*

Responding to people's pain with an exhortation to live properly sometimes reflects an uncaring heart and a shallow view of sin. People who deeply care and who richly understand sin as more than wrong actions will compassionately but relentlessly expose the problem in such a way that forgiveness, not moral commitment, is seen as the necessary beginning of a solution.

The tendency in modern Christianity is to recommend either *external morality* or *self-development* as the path to abundant living. And we thereby miss the point altogether.

Until we see self-centeredness as the core obstacle in the way of mature Christian living that neither moralistic effort nor personal growth can remove, we will continue to devote our energies to solving lesser problems. Rather than coming to understand how God can in fact change us into more other-centered people by first forgiving our selfishness, and thus promoting a deep joy that can survive any crisis, we worry more about changing the painful things in our lives.

## What Would Make Us Truly Happy?

It would be an interesting exercise to ask a group of Christian people to write down what they think they need right now, more than anything else, to make them truly happy.

Some, I suspect, would put at the top of their list a closer walk with the Lord. A majority of these, I further suspect, would have on their minds more consistency in spiritual disciplines such as Bible study and prayer. Others would write down social justice in the church and at home. Still others, I think the majority, would turn to the painful struggles in their immediate circumstances and record needs such as these:

- a husband who would stop drinking
- a more sexually interested wife
- a medical report that the tissue is benign
- a better job
- more money
- a man to marry
- an estranged son coming home
- a rebellious daughter straightening out
- a husband or wife or parent or child coming to Christ

These concerns are deeply felt, both in the hearts of the listmakers and in the heart of God.

And each one brings pain into our lives that won't go away until someone else or something outside of ourselves changes. It is right and good to pray fervently that God would make the change we desire.

But each of these responses is a wrong answer to the question, what do I need *more than anything else* to make me deeply happy? There is only one correct answer: forgiveness from God that brings me into relationship with him and ongoing forgiveness that makes continued fellowship possible. Every other answer is wrong.

If we had asked, *other* than forgiveness, what do I need right now to make me happy, then many of the above answers could be quite correct. We tend, however, to define our problems, at least our currently most pressing ones, in such a way that something other than forgiveness is seen as our greatest need. But this tendency reflects our darkened understanding of life.

Without the power of forgiveness operating in my life right now, even as I write this sentence, I remain alone and unloved, uncared for by anyone who is fully committed to my well-being, locked into an existence with no point, "tired of living and scared of dying," capable of enjoying only those pleasures that mask reality and afterward increase my sense of emptiness, and afraid to face the awful freedom of choosing my way in the dark.

Somehow, and it is a tribute to the ingenuity of devilish wisdom, we manage to believe that we do not really need continued forgiveness. We may give forgiveness its preeminent place in public confession, but privately we're quite persuaded that something else is really more vital to our lives. Forgiveness seems more important as a once laid foundation for our lives than as a presently and continually needed reality. Forgiveness *begins* the Christian life, but, we assume, something else (moral effort? self development?) sustains it. And whatever it is, we pursue with evangelistic fervor, and thus continue on in an essentially self-centered approach to life.

Relationship with God established *and maintained* by his forgiveness provides the only framework within which we can be concerned with our own well-being without being wrongly self-centered. And this is because entering into that relationship, and learning to enjoy it more deeply, requires that we depend not on our own efforts to gain life or to protect ourselves from pain but rather on whatever a kind God chooses to do as we repentantly follow him. John Piper, in *Desiring God*, describes a similar idea that he calls Christian hedonism and rightly commends it.

When we move from an indifference about our selfishness to a convicting awareness of it, an awareness that makes forgiveness more important to us right now than anything else we can imagine, then we are on the road to building good relationships. But how do we make that move?

## ONLY GOD'S LAW CAN SHATTER OUR EXCUSES

People hurt. All of us do. We were designed to live in a far better world than the one we now inhabit. In the better world yet ahead for God's family, we will care deeply about one another. Complaining will be as foreign to our purified natures as disease to our then perfect bodies.

In this world, things are not that way. We are lonely. We are wounded by rejection, angered by cruelty, disillusioned by power-hungry Christian leaders, exhausted by endless responsibilities, saddened by distance from loved ones, confused and hurt by family tensions, grieved beyond words by the suffering of a terminally ill child, and troubled to the point of breakdown by upsetting changes in our lives.

Both the godly and the ungodly seem to enjoy the opportunities of life, despite its trials. Godly people joyfully delight in good things—a tasty meal, a weekend away, the company of friends—and nobly endure hard things—an anorexic daughter, a layoff, betrayal by a friend. They know that their existence is meaningful and that they are destined for unlimited pleasure at the deepest level. Because they keenly feel that nothing now quite meets the standards of their longing souls, the quiet but deeply throbbing ache within them drives them not to complaint, but to anticipation and further yieldedness.

The difference between godly and ungodly people is not that one group never hurts and the other group does, or that one reports more happiness than the other. The difference lies in what people do with their hurt. Either they do what comes naturally: use their hurt to justify self-centered efforts to relieve it, caring less about how they affect others and more about whether they are comfortable; or they do what comes *unnaturally*: use their hurt to better understand and encourage others while they cling desperately to the Lord for promised deliverance, passionately determined to do his will.*

The best of us sometimes yield to the tendency to justify a consuming interest in ourselves. Our thoughts run along these lines:

> Anyone who knew what I've endured and how hard I work to just keep my head above water, and how bad I sometimes feel, would take a noncritical interest in me and try to help. My situation really does justify my thinking more about how I'm making it than worrying about you and your problems.
>
> When we're together, I feel hurt when you don't ask many questions about how things are going for me. Well, yes, I don't ask much about you, that's true, and I'm sure I should be more interested in you, but I've had such a time with my kids. One of mine is still home all day, you know; yours are all in school, aren't they?
>
> And did you know our newer car (it's three years old) is in for repairs again? By the way, I do like the new one you're driving. And the carpet man said he couldn't install our new carpets for two more weeks. It's just one thing after the other.
>
> Oh, did I tell you that we're not going to be able to get away for Christmas and my parents aren't able to come here either? Sometimes I wonder if my kids even know they have grandparents . . .

---

*Godly living can be said to be natural to a Christian in that it is consistent with the desire to please God present in every regenerated heart.

We are so easily caught up in ourselves. It comes so naturally. When we prattle on about our lives in a mood of "I've got it harder than anybody else," no one really listens, and all but the most seasoned prattlers sense that any display of interest from others is at best polite.

We end these doleful conversations feeling uncared for, believing that our friends are selfishly insensitive. The thought of reaching out to *them* seems unbearable; they should come to us to prove their friendship.

Justified self-centeredness is such an automatic and well-practiced premise for our thinking about relationships that only the hammer of God's law can break it apart. And it does so in an unexpected way.

Most of us would prefer to think of God warmly cheering us on as we try to keep our balance in the storms of life. And God does deeply encourage. But something in *our* character brings out another part of his, making him less the cheerleader rooting us to victory and more the determined surgeon wielding a knife.

He sees in us what we, with eyes marred by convenient blind spots, fail to recognize. We think our deepest struggles are coping with a disagreeable spouse or finding a snatch of comfort in a terribly uncomfortable world. But God sees the cancer of self-centeredness that has tainted our most patient and heroic deeds. In keeping with his relentless concern for our perfect health, he hangs copies of the alarming X-rays all about our room, intending to make us aware of our desperate condition.

But we look away, governed by the mistaken idea that someone who understood our hurt would respond with only sympathy and support. Meanwhile, God, who understands even those hurts that we've forgotten, continues to discourage us with reminders of our failure to love perfectly, refusing to bend even an inch in his demand for perfection.

The law of God is relentlessly rigid. It never gives anyone a break because no one, regardless of what he or she has suffered, *deserves* a break. Total other-centeredness is required of us at every moment, whether in the presence of a caring friend or an unfaithful spouse. The slightest compromise with purity ends any hope of acceptance by God. People who present the quality of their lives to God as grounds for relationship with him will instead be removed from his presence.

Creatures like us, who are so prone to excusing our lack of love for others by reminding ourselves how poorly others love us, need to see that God, even when we hurt the most, commands us to respond with unstained love.

But he doesn't *expect* us to; in fact, he knows that we won't. His inflexible commandments are intended to acquaint us with another dimension of his character: his grace, a dimension only those who have failed and admitted it can enjoy.

Our choice then, once we admit we cannot do all that we're told to do, becomes *either* to call the law bad (and to prepare our defense for the day when we're summoned to the eternal court by listing every injury that we've sustained from life) *or* to admit that is we who are bad.

Now admitting we're bad is quite another matter

from despising who we are. Many of us vaguely sense that we are not quite what we should be. But often, this discomfort is an illegitimate disdain for ourselves that developed when imperfect authorities in our lives used impossible standards of behavior to reject us.

It is thoroughly proper to desire escape from the dark night of mean-spirited rejection into the brightness of God's accepting grace. But often the route of escape takes us first through an even darker night, where we stand alone before a fair judge, forced to admit that his anger toward us is a deserved response to our real failure.

## The Proper Attitude: Humble Confession

The ongoing attitude of the maturing self-aware Christian is one of humble confession: "Lord, at every moment of my life, regardless of the hurt I experience, your law condemns me. Your standards are right, but I cannot meet them. I am not good enough to do what you require. I am worthy of judgment. Forgiveness is my deepest need right now and will continue to be my deepest need till I die. Because your atoning death meets that need, I can live in the freedom of forgiveness, neither obsessed with my sin nor indifferent toward it."

God could randomly select any five-minute slice from our lives and, after evaluating our thoughts, motives, and deeds during this brief period, *justly* throw us into outer darkness to wander forever alone in agony and despair. When we begin to grasp this, our excuses appear weak and our selfishness deadly. We are then on our way to enjoying grace and to becoming more other-centered.

When we hear the demands of the law repeated

with firm insistence during even our hardest times, our excuses for self-centeredness are shattered. We can *then* hear the whispers of his love: "You're forgiven. Everything's OK. Enjoy!" Not our efforts to be more loving but God's forgiveness is the foundation for everything good that we bring to our relationships.

Perhaps a simple example will make the point.

A husband and wife are wandering the aisles of a grocery store together, she in the lead, he pushing the cart behind her. He did not want to come, but his wife (for reasons unclear to him) expressed a strong desire for his company. So, feeling noble, he agreed to come.

Stopping in front of a large display of spices, the wife methodically scans each row. Cumin, coriander, cloves, cream of tartar. He wonders why the search is taking so long and asks, with poorly concealed impatience, "What are you looking for?" She inarticulately mutters the name of a spice he would not recognize if clearly pronounced.

He feels a sudden surge of irritability. "What do you need it for anyway? I'm really getting hungry."

Throwing him a withering look of disbelief, she snaps back, "I don't know why I asked you to come," and tears off down the aisle, hurt and angry.

Suppose, just after the spice was incoherently pronounced and the husband first became aware of his impatience, he had thought to himself, "I'm really annoyed that she's taking more time than seems necessary to look for one special spice. I know I'm feeling a bit noble for agreeing to come; I was tired after a long day at work. I feel that she really ought to be sensitive to my fatigue and appreciative that I came and, therefore, move faster. I'm asking her to look out for me. But God wants me to use this opportunity to somehow encourage her. Anything less than a genuine desire to bless her, and actions consistent with this purpose deserves judgment."

## Three Possible Responses

If the husband thought along these lines, he might react in one of three ways. He might feel *enraged* that God would require him to be kind to her when he has already done more than his share of good deeds. "It's not fair that I be required to look out for her right now. It's my turn to be kindly treated." He then might poke her with the cart to move her along. The apostle Paul speaks of God's law arousing our sinful passions (Rom. 7:5).

Second, he might *commit himself to do better.* Rather than admitting that he simply is not capable of loving her in that moment (or any other) with the perfect love God requires, he determines to treat her well. But when he realizes that God requires him to treat her *perfectly* from a thoroughly willing heart controlled completely by love for her, then he despairs. He already broke his commitment when his selfish heart became irritated over a moment of inconvenience. The only way to keep his commitment is to lower God's standards to a level he can meet. And then, if he meets them, he will become proud.

There is a third possible response: he might admit his inability to do what is right, be shamed by his tendency to excuse an unkind reaction to his wife, and *plead for mercy*. This is the only one of the three choices that will lead the husband to other-centeredness. God gives standards not first of all to teach us how to live, but to convince us that we can't meet them. We simply aren't good enough. It isn't only that we're weak. We are *selfish*, more interested in ourselves than anyone else. The third choice puts the husband in reach of God's trans-forming grace and makes possible humble efforts to treat his wife well.

We can stand before God, equipped with all our excuses, and he, fully understanding those excuses, still pronounces us guilty. The vision of this scene must become imbedded in our thinking, strength-ened by studying what God says in his Word about sin, reinforced by honest feedback from our friends and spouse about the ways in which we act self-ishly, and nourished by reflection on these selfish thoughts and feelings and our excuses for them.

The more we realize that our performance, even as mature Christians, will never reach the level of perfection needed to avoid his wrath, the more our excuses for sin will shatter under the weight of fear. And we will enter into a despair that only the kindness of God can relieve.

## CHANGE OCCURS IN THE CONTEXT OF HOPE

This may sound strange, but listening to God's law makes possible, as nothing else does, for me to see the kindness in his heart.

More than two hundred years ago, Jonathan Edwards expressed a similar thought:

Seek that you may see that you are utterly undone, and that you cannot help yourself; and yet, that you do not deserve that God should help you, and that He would be perfectly just if He should refuse to ever help you. If you have come to this, then you will be prepared for comfort. When persons are thus humble, it is God's manner soon to comfort them."[1]

Removing excuses for sin creates an awareness of our most basic need—forgiveness—but by itself does not draw us to God. If matters are left there, we are in an awful mess.

But understanding how completely we deserve judgment, even for impatience by a spice rack, helps us to see why God delays in administering it. If God's law expresses his character, then surely he is never indifferent to our sin. His delay in meting out justice rather reflects his patience. He does not want anyone to perish, but everyone to repent (2 Peter 3:9).

For Christians, those of us who have already trusted Christ for salvation, it is humbling to realize that God's patience makes possible for us to understand our sin more thoroughly and to learn deeper levels of both repentance and joy.

Take the husband by the spice rack, for example. The man described in the incident was converted to Christ more than thirty-five years ago. I know, because I am he.

I can be confronted with the continuing sinfulness of my heart, realize that my only hope is forgiveness, and then, conscious that where sin abounds, grace abounds even more, begin to sense the welcome movement of God's Spirit, prompting me to deal gently with Rachael, my wife. Now my determination to do right involves a passionate warmth toward Rachael. Obedience becomes less a mechanical choice and more a wanted direction.

It may take years, but facing the requirements of God in a way that shatters our excuses for self-centered living and becoming aware of his forgiveness will lead to surprising evidence of change.

No one turns to someone who condemns. A walk to the courthouse is never pleasant for one whose speeding was accurately registered by radar. But, once condemned, we long to find someone who forgives. Once we understand the extent of God's judgment, our longing for forgiveness becomes literally the most intense desire of our condemned hearts, crowding out all those lesser desires for pleasure, fame, or merely human companionship. Nothing matters more to the person trapped in a burning house than getting out.

The mystery, of course, is that the one who completely condemns is the same one who completely forgives. God is both holy and loving. But we cannot enjoy his love until we are first crushed by the weight of his holiness. To put it another way, we have no interest in his forgiveness until we see our need of it. The more we become aware of how thoroughly self-centered we are, the more important and wonderful his forgiveness becomes.

Proud people have no sense of impending judgment. They expect compliments and thereby never learn of God's forgiving grace. Humble people, however, meet God in all his wonder as an unbending judge whose heart of love has found a way to forgive them and to restore them to relationship with himself.

When we in our sin meet God in his grace—this does the most to change us. And an ongoing encounter with God, in which we further probe the depths of his forgiveness, not by sinning more but by recognizing more of our sin, continues the process of change.

When more than anything else we long for forgiveness, we then learn to celebrate forgiveness as the foundation of our lives. His grace, not our effort, becomes everything. And as we value God's grace more, we change from self-centered people who angrily yearn for relief from hurt to other-centered people who celebrate his forgiveness by longing to know him better and to make him better known. Change is not only possible for, but also promised to, the Christian who believes that God is the rewarder of those who diligently seek him.

The core dynamic behind all change from self-centeredness to other-centeredness is an appreciation of God's grace. Many forces promote change: admitting self-pity and behaving responsibly can lift depression; sorting through issues of control may relieve eating compulsions; talking sensibly to yourself during a crisis can quiet anxiety. But only one force can move us toward that radically other-centered character of Christ: the celebration of forgiveness.

# Six

## Celebrating Forgiveness

*We may indeed through introspection grow to despise and hate ourselves, but God is greater and more generous than our petty selves and He is far more truly loving and understanding than we can imagine. I am quite certain that He does not want us to waste any time raking over our sins. He wants us to accept His forgiveness and walk forward confidently in His strength.*

J. B. PHILIPS

As I thought about writing this book, I planned to tackle questions about masculinity and femininity right away. I began reading with an intuitive conviction that the differences between men and women run deep and that partners in the best marriages enjoy these differences.

My background reading included material from both the egalitarian and traditional camps. As I became better acquainted with both perspectives, I became increasingly concerned that neither side was dealing adequately with the loathsome and deeply entrenched problem of self-centeredness, the thing that interferes with getting along more than either refusing to fit into roles or refusing to break out of them.

The traditional camp is often heard as favoring a

military-style arrangement in which submissive wives do what they're told by decisive men. I did not want to write a book that encouraged men and women to squeeze into clearly defined roles with no thought of freely becoming and warmly giving all that God designed them to be and to give.

It is much too easy to maintain order in relationships at the expense of passion. Order in everything, including marriage, is necessary and good, but biblical order *promotes* rather than *dampens* our enjoyment of one another. And does so by drawing on our commitment to give who we are for the sake of the other.

I therefore felt cautious about emphasizing sex-related roles that encourage conformity to a standard more than opportunities to uniquely love.

I struggled, too, with the egalitarian alternative to hierarchical order in marriage. I sympathized with the substance (though not always the tone) of this camp's fierce insistence that male supremacy and female servility represent a damaging distortion of biblical data, but I was bothered by the understanding of freedom that seemed implicit in much of its literature.*

Christian feminists seem to begin with an anti-authority bias that defines hierarchy in human relationships as bad in itself rather than regarding

---

*Donald Bloesch sums up my viewpoint well. He says that, according to feminist theology, God "enables both men and women to realize their full potential as sons and daughters of a new age in which sexual differences are no longer a barrier to . . . spiritual leadership." Feminist theology, Bloesch continues, mirrors "the new wave of democratic egalitarianism that seeks to eradicate all hierarchy in human relationships" (Donald Bloesch, *Freedom for Obedience* [San Francisco: Harper & Row, 1987], 266-67).

an *improper use* of authority as bad. Because men and women are equally human and equally valuable, they argue, the idea of male authority over females is demeaning to women and inconsistent with the equal status of both sexes before God. The important thing is to become more aware of your dignity and to express it more fully. A marriage between equals, they teach, will build on a foundation of mutually recognized and honored dignity.

The egalitarian idea of freedom seems to shift the focus *away from* living according to divine plan *toward* realizing personal potential. The difference in these two conceptions of freedom is enormous. The former directly confronts selfishness, the latter treats it as a secondary problem.

The first order of business, in egalitarian thinking, is to come alive with the dignity of equal personhood. Defining freedom in terms of realized human potential recasts God as a divine enabler, dedicated to helping us push back the limits of personal boundaries and more fully enjoy our humanness. His identity as sovereign Lord and gracious Redeemer becomes vague, still acknowledged as foundational, perhaps, but no longer continually relevant to our most pressing concerns.

More personally, the emphasis on marriage as a partnership between equals left me strangely unwarmed. Certainly my wife, Rachael, is a person of equal value, but more important, she is enjoyably different. Learning to express our differences with the other's well-being in mind seems a far warmer ambition than asserting mutual equality. Something wonderfully possible between husband and wife seems to be missing in the egalitarian framework.

Neither traditionalists nor egalitarians adequately highlight the central problem of self-centeredness in marriage. Fitting into roles can provoke self-serving conformity, and affirming equal value can encourage self-serving assertiveness. And when we lightly regard the stubborn sin of selfishness, when either obedient conformity or asserted dignity seems an adequate solution to our relationship problems, then we will not properly value the deep work of God in forgiving our selfishness and changing us into giving people.

## THE PERVASIVENESS OF SELF-CENTEREDNESS

When I grasp even feebly the subtle and stubborn pervasiveness with which, even during a casual conversation, I selfishly arrange for my own well-being, then God's command to redirect my energies to promoting someone else's welfare is overwhelming. It requires a change in the most firmly rooted parts of my nature. Trying to obey his command in its fullness is like a paralytic attempting to stand or a lung cancer victim working hard to not cough.

When I reflect on what God tells me to do, I must immediately admit defeat. I'm just not good enough to meet his standards. When I face how naturally self-centered I am, the goal of obedience seems hopelessly beyond reach. To ask God for further opportunities for self-expression would be monstrously inappropriate. I am reduced to needing first forgiveness, then help to obey.

All clear thinking about relationships between

men and women depends on a growing awareness of how wrongly committed we are to looking after ourselves, an awareness that makes forgiveness in Christ the central and most relished fact about life. Gratitude for the ongoing reality of forgiveness is the soil in which a desire to live as we were designed grows and develops. Or, to put the same thought another way, realizing that we never mature beyond our need of forgiving grace is the basis of all our maturing.

Nothing is more basic to Christian living than our celebration of this forgiveness. There is far more to ponder and appreciate than forgiveness; other truths about Christ can inflame us with passion to know him better. But nothing must ever be allowed to replace our gratitude for redemption.

And other-centered relating, the most crucial element in building a marriage, will develop only where husbands and wives value forgiveness as the most necessary element in their lives. This central point can be emphasized first by defining a *good* relationship, and then by describing what I mean by celebrating forgiveness.


## DEFINING A GOOD RELATIONSHIP

Most of us are at least vaguely aware that *things* don't bring us lasting happiness. Experience has taught us (or is trying to) that the good feelings generated by a new dress, a trip to the Orient, a house on the beach, dinner at the Ritz Carlton, or a promotion to vice president are neither deep nor lasting.

The simple truth is that true happiness cannot exist apart from personal relationship. At some level, we all know this. But if we have never tasted real joy through another person, we may find ourselves addicted to good feelings and miserably enslaved to shallow pleasures.

For too many, however, the relationships that are supposed to bring the most happiness serve up the worst misery. Tensions with parents, frustrations with children, and angry distance between spouses sometimes make shallow pleasure seem preferable.

Because family relationships are sometimes more painful than satisfying, many people manage to find someone outside of their family with whom time together feels good. Lonely wives talk at length with special women friends. Frustrated husbands enjoy golf with a good buddy, and meaningful relationships with someone of the opposite sex often develop. We want to feel connected with somebody, to share with someone who understands and cares, to be with someone who lets us go off duty and relax. *It feels so good to enjoy who we are in someone else's presence.*

And when we are with that someone, it is entirely natural to think of this relationship as good. But notice how the word *good* gets defined: a good relationship, in this natural way of thinking, is one that provides us with whatever we need to feel happy. Using this definition, a happily married couple could call their relationship good for precisely the same reason adulterous lovers might value theirs. In both situations, people feel good about themselves in the presence of another.

Something is clearly wrong with a definition of good relationships that can be claimed by both committed spouses and immoral roommates.

Part of the problem with our understanding of what makes a relationship good is that we start with the wrong data. Finding couples who seem to be happy and looking at their relationships to sort out the ingredients for successful relating is risky. A fallen world filled with deceived people who often feel good for wrong reasons is no place to do our research. We may as well formulate moral principles by studying the mating habits of animals.

## The Only Example of Perfect Relating

To understand what good relationship is we need to consider the only example of perfect relating: God. It is legitimate to question how the three Persons of the Godhead manage to get along so well. Certainly they never quarrel. We never read of the Spirit getting jealous of the Son's top billing. When they met in committee to discuss creation, no decision had to be tabled due to bickering over what should be created first or who would do what.

If it's true that two's company and three's a crowd, one might expect that in all the years they've been together some trouble would have developed. Most couples can't make it through their first night without fussing about something.

Such talk, of course, is nonsense and, if I were serious, blasphemous. But it does point up that relationships within the Trinity are very different from ours. Their way of relating is so radically right that God the Father, God the Son, and God the Holy Spirit, in some mysterious but profoundly meaningful way, can be regarded as one.

But what does their manner of relating have to do with developing a definition of good relationships among mere mortals?

Just before he died, our Lord was reflecting on the closeness he enjoyed with his Father. Perhaps he was prompted by the recent memory of James and John's jockeying for position among the twelve, or of Peter's pledging superior loyalty when things got tough. He turned his eyes upward and with a heart filled with joy and longing said, "I pray also for those who will believe in me . . . that all of them may be one, Father, just as you are in me and I am in you" (John 17:20—21).

In that prayer, our Lord set before us the standard for measuring a good relationship. Theologian D. Broughton Knox expressed it this way: "The doctrine of the trinity tells us that ultimate reality is personal relationship" and that ". . . the characteristic of true relationship is other-person-centeredness."[1]

Consider just a few samples of trinitarian relating. The Father loves the Son (John 3:35). He shows him all that he does (John 5:20). The Son in response always does what pleases the Father (John 8:29), and his obedience springs from his love for his Father (John 14:31). The Spirit is self-effacing. He does not speak of himself, but he takes the things of the Son and shows them to believers. He glorifies Christ (John 16:13—14).[2]

Beginning with the data of divine relationships rather than our experiences with each other, we can come close to defining a good relationship. A good relationship is one in which *each member willingly and actively devotes whatever he or she has to give to the well-being of the other*. In such a relationship, the highest criterion for deciding what to do at any moment is a person's understanding before God of what would be the greatest service he or she can offer to the other.

When *good* is thus defined, the focus is put where it belongs, on the *giving* of self rather than either the *development* of self or the *conformity* of self to imposed standards. Neither self-expression nor fitting into roles are the marks of a good relationship.

Thinking about a good relationship in this way provides real comfort and hope to godly folks married to difficult spouses. If, for example, a husband devotes himself to actively loving his angry wife, then regardless of her indifference to his care and her continued hardness, we can fairly say that *his relationship to her* (or his style of relating to her) satisfies the definition of "good."

*Her relationship to him,* of course, is bad, and similarly *their relationship with each other* cannot be called good. But the faithful spouse experiences both *joy* in remaining true to ultimate goodness and *sorrow* in enduring cold rejection, the sorrow our Lord feels at every moment. Surely this is an example of sharing in the fellowship of his suffering, a welcome opportunity for someone who can say, more than anything else, "I want to know Christ" (Phil. 3:10).

Good relating to others, defined as other-centeredness after the pattern of the Trinity, is the core fruit of Christian living. All Bible study that gets at what God is saying will have some impact on how we relate. If it doesn't, then we are simply gaining knowledge that puffs up.

Whatever conclusions we reach about the uniqueness of men and women and how they should relate to each other must reflect, above all else, a passionate determination to do something for the other in response to what God has done for them. This is the mark of good relating.

## WHAT IT MEANS TO CELEBRATE FORGIVENESS

Clearly, if I am to learn what it means to be a godly man, I must do something about my natural tendency to worry more about me than about you. I earlier suggested that the relentless standards of God can expose my self-centeredness as inexcusably wrong but that only an appreciation of the kindness of God would draw me to repentance and lead to real change. I now want to take that discussion a step further and talk about the celebration of God's kindness as the basis for continuing growth in other-centeredness.

I have made clear, I trust, that self-centeredness is not simply a wrong turn that can be easily corrected. Shifting from a primary concern for me to a primary concern for you never happens naturally, nor do I have the power to make it happen by sheer effort. If I am to be transformed into a person who more and more values my life as an opportunity for service, then grace will have to impact me so strongly and deeply that it shatters my self-commitment and replaces it with genuine concern for others.

But so often we're moved by lesser things than grace.

A simple illustration will explain. I wrote most of this book during an extended stay in England. During this time Rachael and I had the opportunity to see several plays in London theaters. At different moments we laughed, we cried, we felt excited, we were saddened, we became enraged. We were struck, as we often are after being well entertained, how mere human fiction or well-performed music can move us more deeply than divine drama.

Somehow we manage to miss the breathtaking reality of the Christian story. The truth of that drama should be more incredibly and wonderfully shocking than the most imaginative ending to a mystery ever thought up by Agatha Christie.

But when it isn't, when our commitment to self-centeredness remains lodged in a part of our souls that nothing has yet disturbed, our efforts to be good to one another feel like programmed hypocrisy, choices that we sometimes make out of a sense of duty, rather than out of a passionate desire to be more loving. We may wish the gospel moved us more, but we have to admit that we sometimes respond with more passion to a good play than to a good sermon.

And God's work in us is thwarted when we fail to catch the excitement of what he's doing in our lives.

Yet the gospel, the good news of forgiveness, more than anything else, is worth celebrating. Biblical Christianity, like good drama, tells a story, a true one, that catches us off guard with its utterly surprising ending. And, as in the best mystery novels, when the surprise ending is revealed, it becomes wonderfully obvious in a way that still staggers and thrills.

As the biblical drama begins, God is introduced as a benevolent Creator, kindly and personally involved with the man and woman he created. But in a moment of bizarre and wicked insanity the man and woman turn away from God to follow someone deceitful and self-serving.

From this beginning, the story proceeds to expose the insolent stupidity of this decision to rebel against God. It details all the misery and trouble this choice brought into the lives of the man and woman, as well as into the lives of their descendants who consistently follow in their first parents' foolish footsteps.

Again and again, God calls them back to himself, but they never come to stay. The narrative makes clear that God is no indulgent grandfather who does little else than patiently sigh over his grandchildren's misbehavior. He is rather a holy judge, who declares that his people's insolence is a capital offense, a heinous crime worthy of death.

There seems no doubt that God will end history by banishing his rebellious creatures into eternal darkness—into community with their hateful master, where self-centeredness reigns supreme. But just as the gavel descends, the Judge stops the proceedings. His stern countenance relaxes into a smile. He now uncorks the Big Surprise.

"I forgive you," he declares. "The blood of my Son covers everything you've done wrong. More than that, it covers every natural urge within you to do wrong. You are fully forgiven. Welcome into the relationship you were designed to enjoy but could never find. Your job is simply to admit you're wrong, to place your confidence in my Son's blood, and to accept my invitation to get to know me better. Everything else is up to me."

That's the story. And when a sinner understands what has happened, he is stunned. Swiss theologian

Emil Brunner has said, "Forgiveness is the very opposite of anything which can be taken for granted. Nothing is less obvious than forgiveness."[3]

It's one thing, of course, to write about forgiveness with words designed to provoke the stunned reaction we are supposed to feel. *It's quite another thing to actually be stunned.*

I wonder if the drama of redemption sometimes seems commonplace because we tend to move too quickly from the reality of self-centeredness to questions that we find more compelling precisely because we are self-centered. Do we react to the gospel with only casual appreciation because we concern ourselves with Christian living in a way that reduces issues of sin and grace to merely an historical foundation, an act of kindness a loving parent did years ago?

Is possible that the energy with which we study the biblical text to develop and defend our views on marital relating is more self-oriented than God-pursuing? Could we really be so deceived that the passion we feel as we articulate and promote whatever we're persuaded the Bible teaches springs more from personal bias than from the Spirit's guidance?

When we lose touch with the continuing reality of our selfishness, then forgiveness becomes something that is good of God to do, like the newspaper carrier's making sure the morning edition lands under the porch on a rainy day. We feel moved enough to remember his kindness with a generous tip the next time he collects.

Part of the problem is that we feel the *reality of our wounds* more than the *fact of our sin.* We therefore react with more passion to those things that restore a sense of personal wholeness than to our redemption.

How wrong of us to dedicate our energy to becoming whole. History is filled with the lives of godly men and women who managed to bless others in the midst of unrelieved personal struggles that left them feeling anything but whole.

Everything we do has a deeply personal agenda. And those agendas are shaped by our determination to survive in a world that hurts and offends us.[4] Sanctification includes abandoning every agenda that aims toward recovering or enhancing our own intactness, and pursuing God with not our wholeness, but with his glory, in view, with the confidence that his agenda includes satisfying every longing in our hearts.

To progress in true holiness, we need to cultivate a continuing sensitivity to self-centeredness that makes gratitude to a forgiving God far more real than an eagerness to see others agree with our views. When the place of women in the church and home becomes more divisive than puzzling, when the passion we feel as we discuss our views is more concerned with intensely convincing than with warmly blessing, then it is time to look away from our arguments to the motives beneath them. And if we look honestly and deeply, we will find self-serving agendas that make forgiveness seem less vital to our souls' well-being than progress toward a desired end.

Nothing is wrong, of course, in doing what we can to resolve our battles with depression and self-doubt, but it is wrong to shift our focus *away from* celebrating forgiveness by living other-centered lives *to* finding a path to personal healing. We exist for God; he does not exist for us. We must keep our attention riveted on the core issues of the gospel.

If the beginning of the gospel is the message of

judgment (see Rom. 1:1—3:20), then the heart of the gospel is the wonder of forgiveness. When sin is realized and the gospel embraced, then forgiveness is celebrated. We need not artificially induce a joyful mood. Even when the confusion and heartaches of life shake us badly and we feel more like weeping or lashing out than singing (and those seasons come often on the path to maturity), forgiveness serves as our anchor.

As we celebrate forgiveness, sometimes with singing and sometimes with a determined awareness of its centrality in our life, other-centeredness develops. It is the Spirit's work. The growing realization, against everything we naturally think, that our *selfishness*, more than our hurt, is an obstacle to joy creates the momentum for giving up self-serving agendas and for going about the business of living with the well-being of others in view. The center of the gospel, unsurprisingly, is the center of all growth in becoming like Christ.

I have suggested that the *beginning* of the gospel is the message of judgment and that the *core* of the gospel is forgiveness through Christ's shed blood.

Although it is not my purpose in this book, I want to make clear that there is more to the good news of Christ than the reality of forgiveness. When God forgives a sinner, he welcomes him into a relationship that includes a wealth of blessing: union with Christ; an indwelling Holy Spirit; the advocacy of a Great High Priest; a new heart that desires to please God, delights in his Word, and loves his people. The list goes on and on.

At the time of our redemption, we became a new creation, complete with an identity that frees us to relate as sons and daughters of God because

Christ is now in us, the hope of glory (Col. 1:27). When our Lord prayed for his own, he asked his Father to sanctify all who would follow him by the truth (John 17:17). Certainly that truth extends beyond the central truth of forgiveness.

The message of redemption, the forgiveness of sins (Col. 1:14), is the foundation of our relationship with God, but ushers us into further truths about God and our relationship with him that we must grasp if we are to progress in purity.

I would not want my emphasis on forgiveness to suggest that nothing more needs to be understood in our walk toward holy living. Perhaps I can summarize my thinking this way: first the law, then forgiveness, and then the riches of Christ that free us to walk more and more worthily of our calling.

Self-centered living is the real culprit in marriages with problems. Other-centered living is the answer. Understanding how badly we need forgiveness and celebrating its rich availability moves us in the right direction.

We are now ready to ask the next question, whether other-centered living in men differs from other-centered living in women. When a man lovingly relates to his wife, will he do anything distinctly masculine that would be unnatural for his wife to do? Does a woman who loves her husband with other-centered energy behave differently from a man when he loves well?

What are the differences between men and women, and how does learning to give up our selfishness free us to enjoy them? These are the concerns of the rest of the book.

# Part Two

HOW RELATIONSHIPS
DO WORK:
THE DIFFERENCE
MEN AND WOMEN
CAN ENJOY

# *Seven*

## A Tough Question

*The thief who is trying to be better is ages ahead of the most honorable man who is making no such effort.*

GEORGE MACDONALD

*Mike and Debby have been married for nineteen years.* Mike works as a mechanic at an auto repair shop; Debby is a homemaker. They have two children, Todd, 17, and Amy, 14.

They are going through some rough times right now. Mike's biweekly paycheck doesn't quite stretch two weeks, and Todd, their teenage son, is acting out. A few months ago Todd was arrested for drunken driving. A few days ago Mike discovered a small plastic bag of marijuana under the front seat of Todd's Ford Escort. He didn't tell Debby what he found.

Mike can tell that Debby is feeling the strain. Little things that she used to joke about—towels on the bathroom floor, a basement light left on, the newspaper carrier missing the porch step—now irritate her. The dinner hour, formerly a time of playful banter and sharing, is now charged with tension. Just last night Debby ran in tears from the table.

Mike worries that Debby is slipping into depression and doesn't want to make things worse. He can't forget the look of anguish on her face when she learned of Todd's arrest. If she knew about the marijuana, it might destroy her. Should he tell her? Or is it better to bear the burden alone? What could he do that would encourage Debby, really encourage her? What does she want that he could give?

Meanwhile Debby, who handles the household bills, worries about their money problems. When she mentions their strained budget, Mike either snaps at her about spending too much or retreats into an angry sulk. His defensiveness hurts her deeply and further drains her energy to carry on with everyday chores. She knows how hard Mike works for what he earns, and she feels bad, but she doesn't know what to do.

Should she insist Mike sit down with her to hear the hard facts about income and expenses? Or is it better to continue quietly doing her best, thereby relieving Mike of additional pressure and protecting herself from becoming the object of his frustration? What could she do that would help Mike face their struggles without feeling so threatened? What does Mike want that Debby could give?

We've raised two important questions here: What does Debby want that Mike could give, and what does Mike want that Debby could give?

In order to answer these questions, we must first ask a more basic question. Are there relational differences between men and women that Mike and Debby should take into account in building a marriage relationship? We know that men and women are physically different. But are the differences between men and women limited to anatomy and chemistry and therefore not relevant to deep issues of relating?

Do Mike and Debby need only concern themselves with common principles of kindness, truthfulness, and sensitivity in deciding how to relate to one another? Or does Debby long for something that Mike could give her because he is a man, something that would make her feel alive, secure, relaxed, and warmly feminine? Is Mike built to enjoy something Debby could give him because she is a woman, something that would make Mike feel respected, confident, peaceful, and quietly masculine?

Maybe Mike and Debby are different in relational ways that could be enjoyed!

God created us with distinctly sexual bodies designed to pleasurably and productively fit together. Is it possible that gender distinctiveness runs deeper than physical differences, that men and women have different capacities and desires? Does coming together in personal relationship require the same unique blending required for coming together in physical relationship?

These are tough questions. They are as controversial as they are important.

Because gender distinctiveness is such a "hot" topic, it might be wise to think about the elements that generate the heat before I present my thinking on the subject. It is far too easy for all of us to automatically dismiss a viewpoint with which we differ before we consider its merits, or to accept one we like without studying it.

I believe that men and women are different in important ways that, if understood and honored, can lead to a deep enjoyment of one another. I further believe that every husband, because he is a man, has precisely what his wife longs to receive and that every wife, because she is a woman, has precisely what her husband longs to receive, and that as each partner becomes increasingly other-centered and gives those unique elements to the other, the intimacy God intended will develop.

As you read the preceding paragraphs, how did you react? I imagine some of you appreciated the ideas, others weren't sure how you felt, and still others strongly disagreed. Your reaction was determined, in part by past experience, previous study, serious thought, and careful observation. But still you have a bias, an inclination to agree or disagree for personally motivated reasons.

Before I elaborate on my ideas, I want to reflect briefly on our tendency to prefer one viewpoint over another for personal and sometimes illegitimate reasons, and I want to suggest how we might minimize this tendency and therefore enter into more profitable dialogue about this difficult topic of how men and women differ. In this chapter, I want to suggest that our convictions are sometimes less dependent on biblical study and reasoning and more dependent on our own, sometimes hidden, purposes.

What happens, for example, when a church synod meets to decide its official position on male headship and female submission? More is involved in the discussions than a careful study of relevant texts. Such meetings rarely end with a warm and unanimous consensus that emerges from serious biblical study.

When the more verbal members are of one mind, the matter may be easily settled if the timid dissenters sacrifice their views on the altar of peace at any cost. Sometimes the more mature, after persuading as forcefully as love permits, may graciously yield on points they do not see as central.

But what happens when sincere Christians, neither immature nor timid, honestly differ over matters that each side regards as significant? If church history is a reliable guide, we must face the possibility of a split. Phrases like "let's agree to disagree" and "there can be unity in diversity" carry little weight when competing ideas matter deeply to those who hold them. In a fallen world, where the clearest thinkers at best see dimly, the necessity to honor convictions sometimes requires that we separate.

But when that happens, it is the responsibility of all involved to demonstrate friendship and good will to each other and to a cynical world. Those who *enjoy* separating as an expression of their alleged commitment to truth are Pharisees of the worst kind, and their sinfulness corrupts whatever right doctrines they defend.

Separation over content may be necessary for those holding different views. But, before this is allowed, another issue should be considered first.

It is important, of course, to explore the substance of the disagreement, to present the biblical basis for each position, and to talk about the varying interpretations of difficult texts using every scrap of wisdom and scholarship at our disposal. It is right to consider competing views and to determine the biblical support each one enjoys.

There is a time, however, when the most biblical thing to do is to set aside matters of specific content and to probe deeply into the *personal reasons* that make someone want to maintain a certain view.

## CONSIDERING MOTIVES

It is far easier, of course, never to introduce motivation into the discussion. To do so surfaces a whole new set of tensions. Discussing concerns with the biblical text removes us from direct contact with each other's baser parts and encourages us to think that we are remaining within the boundaries of civilized Christian propriety. But, our self-centered agendas may be controlling our interactions in ways that we refuse to admit.

Discussing motivational matters may, for a time at least, complicate and further inflame our discussions. Among other things, we may open the door to *sloppy thinking* ("Maybe I'm committed to the traditional view because I feel too insecure to become a free woman."); *stinging attack* ("I wonder if you're pushing your ideas to prove that you're worth listening to. I see you as inadequate."); and *counterfeit repentance* ("I think we're all trying to win an argument. At least I know I am. And that's wrong so I'll say no more.").

Thinking about personal factors that incline us more toward one view than another is risky business. Possible abuses are many. But perhaps we can minimize the abuses and maximize the profits of looking inside if we realize that the primary value of looking at our motives is not to straighten them out but rather to face our self-centeredness and to let our twisted motivation reduce us to humility and to meaningfully dependent prayer. Nothing less than *true humility*, the kind that refuses to compromise love as it holds firmly to believed positions, and *dependent prayer*, offered by someone who knows that God reigns even when our understanding of justice is violated, provides an adequate context for debate over troubling differences.

The evangelical world is clearly in the midst of a heated debate over the responsibilities of men and women in the church and home. Large numbers of responsible, competent, and informed Christians think that men and women are significantly different and that these differences are rightly reflected when men assume leadership and women responsively submit. Equally large numbers of responsible, competent, and informed Christians believe that the Bible emphasizes the equality of men and women more than whatever differences may exist, and they see no basis for assigning roles or functions according to gender.

Certainly it is right, whenever Christians differ, to spend more energy in studying the Bible. No one argues with that. But it seems to me that the Bible's emphasis on motives suggests that it is also important to evaluate the *energy* with which we study the text. As I read the literature about the issue, almost all of which is devoted to presenting another slant on already well-researched biblical passages, I can't escape the impression that we need more than further scholarly study.

## A SECOND FOCUS

We need a second focus. Let us first focus on the meaning of the biblical passages that directly address the issue. But let us focus secondly on the *person* studying the Bible, using biblical revelation to help us understand that person. What is going on within the interpreter that might bias his or her study?

We can't argue that a Bible student must clear away all bias before the Word is opened. It's a noble thought, but it cannot be done. If we try to remove all prejudice, and worse, if we think we have succeeded, we only manage to hide from ourselves the more deeply embedded motives that color our interpretation, and we thereby strengthen their control over our thinking.

Although relationships are central in Christian living, they rarely receive the attention they deserve, especially among Bible students. To bring into the open whatever self-serving energy may be involved in Bible study, we should encourage the interpreter to consider a rarely asked question: Are you willing to explore the quality of your relationships to learn more of the humility required to hear God's message?

If the answer to this question is yes, two further questions should follow. First, how aware are you of the impact you have on others who know you well? Second, how willing are you to invite feedback about your impact on others and to regard this feedback as vital to your spiritual health?

Let's take the first question first. I have noticed that few Christians devote serious attention to knowing how others perceive them. Such concerns, they often say, belong to the insecure and emotionally dependent. But if the Scriptures express the mind of a God who longs to restore us to loving community, then it is reasonable to expect that time spent studying his Word should make us more alert to our impact on one another's lives (James 1:19—25).

And yet, time and time again, I hear members of a church staff or Christian organization comment that their committee meetings are ruined more by another member's style of relating (often a strong leader's style) than by any controversial content. And no one dares mention to this person that his or her social impact is troublesome, partly because everyone knows that the offender regards this kind of feedback as too personal, too psychological, or simply irrelevant.

When two people leave a group discussion, the one who thinks discerningly and honestly about how others might have perceived him or her, is far closer to loving well and to hearing the mind of God than the one who hasn't a clue about his social impact. Lack of concern for what others think of us reveals not personal strength, but willful arrogance.

And now the second question. *How willing are you to regard this feedback as vital to your spiritual health?*

It is difficult to profit from someone's absolutely honest comments about how we affect them. And yet my marriage has grown the most during times of soul-threatening pain when Rachael and I clearly faced how we were failing one another.

Some people make a fetish out of sharing and, in the name of honesty, say things that never should be said. A great deal of thoroughly self-centered conversation has occurred under the banner of honest sharing of feelings ("Well, at least I had the courage to say what I really felt"). But even though giving difficult feedback has often been done unwisely and unprofitably, and sometimes has severely damaged a relationship, maturity as relational beings still demands that we be willing to face through candid feedback the bad effects we have on others that in our blindness we would see in no other way.

These two questions begin to get at the often unnoticed but powerful forces that energize our personal agendas as we do our thinking. For example, when my family and friends tell me that I'm pressuring and critical, it is only then that I can glimpse how determined and desperate I am to prove something about myself as I relate to others. If I brace myself to follow the Holy Spirit into the dark regions of my heart (Heb. 4:12; Ps. 139:23, 24; Prov. 20:27) where self-centered thoughts and intents direct my movements more than I want to admit, eventually I am broken, humble, and renewed in my praise for a forgiving God, and more able to hear his voice as I return to my study.

It is this process that best equips us to understand the real thrust of the biblical message about any subject, whether it be prophecy, sin, or men and women, because God's fundamental message is about relationship with him and with others (Matt. 22:37—40). Those directed by self-serving agendas are listening for something else.

Scholarship, without the humility that comes only from an unflattering look at how we relate, breeds not godly wisdom but arrogant knowledge. We will come closer to God's view on difficult subjects like male and female differences when humble people, those who are bothered by how easily and often their style of relating causes damage, share their understanding of the biblical record.

Mounds of technical arguments, tracing the etymology of the Greek word for *head* and researching the cultural situation in which Paul spoke will continue to enjoy a deservedly important place. However, because equally competent scholars can look at the data from different angles and can then draw contradictory conclusions, technical arguments will finally prove compelling only to the folks who already grant their premise.

At a conference held a few years ago to present various viewpoints on male and female differences, biblical scholars made their case for the positions they believed were best supported by the text. After listening to the wealth of arguments, J. I. Packer responded with what strikes me as humble wisdom when he said that certain passages " . . . continue to convince me that the man-woman relationship is intrinsically non-reversible." [1]

I find this statement compelling. Perhaps because Packer is expressing a view I already accept. Or perhaps because his thought strikes me as true because it *is* true. Either could, of course, explain my attraction to Packer's statement. There is no way to decide ultimately which it is. All any of us can do is to continue learning the humility that develops from facing our impact on people and to stay consciously dependent on God's Spirit for wisdom as we remain committed to the Scriptures.

When we meet in committee with ministry partners to think through potentially divisive subjects, we must look at our motivations in the hope that learning to discuss questions with a disarming humility will promote meaningful dialogue.

This is true for both you and me. That's why I wrote the first part of this book first. It represents an effort to promote humility. This part of the book, in which I offer my understanding of masculinity and femininity, is written to people, and I hope I am among them, who pay attention to their effect on others because nothing matters more to them than other-centered relating and because they know that there is nothing more difficult to do.

Men and women who yearn to become more godly men and women make up the audience I most want to reach. When people visibly committed to other-centered relating as measured by their humbling awareness of their social impact react negatively to my thinking, then I must seriously rethink my views. When there are Bible scholars among that group, I will eagerly welcome their evaluation of my ideas in light of their specialized knowledge.

If my thinking is moving in the right direction, toward what is actually true, then it will ring true in the hearts and minds of Christians who value other-centered living far more than they cherish any particular understanding of the differences between men and women.

# *Eight*

## Is There Really a Difference?

*Christianity did not come in order to develop the heroic virtues in the individual but rather to remove self-centeredness and establish love.*

SØREN KIERKEGAARD

*No one quarrels with the observation that men and* women are different, in at least a few noticeable and important ways. And we all agree that these differences equip one sex better for certain tasks than for others. Men, for example, cannot bear children and women can't impregnate men.

Most Christians agree that these physical differences have implications for our relationships. Two men or two women or a man and a woman can share a close friendship, but *romantic* friendship rightly belongs only to a man and a woman. A lifelong commitment that includes sexual intimacy must be heterosexual. A man living with a man and a woman living with a woman in a sexual relationship, no matter how committed they may be to each other, perverts God's design.

But why? If God's prohibition of homosexual

relationships is not merely whimsical, if it reflects the kind intentions of our Maker, then perhaps there is something distinctively masculine about men that was designed to fit with whatever is distinctively feminine about women.

The Bible pushes the issue a step further. "A woman must not wear men's clothing, nor a man wear women's clothing, for the LORD your God detests anyone who does this" (Deut. 22:5).* Although cultures vary in what they regard as male and female clothing, there generally is a clear distinction. In modern Western culture, both men and women wear pants, but women's pants are different from men's pants. God wants men to look like men and women to look like women.

Is there something unique and basic about manhood and womanhood that God wants us to express through our relationships and in our appearance? Does homosexual involvement compromise something essential in our sexual identity? Is there something about a man that is betrayed or violated when he enjoys wearing women's clothing? In other words, is there something we can properly call maleness or femaleness that extends *beyond the body* (its anatomy, chemistry, and clothing) and *into the soul?*

---

*Many hold that this passage teaches a principle that is normative across time and culture forbidding cross-dressing. However, for reasons too involved to discuss in a footnote, some think that this passage (1) prohibits men from impersonating women in order to escape military service and (2) forbids dressing women in soldiers' clothing and then placing them in the front lines of battle. If, in fact, this verse has less to do with cross-dressing than with male cowardice, regarding cross-dressing as wrong is still a fair conclusion from other biblical teaching on sexual distinctiveness (Rom. 1:26—27).

The debate begins when someone insists that *men and women differ in ways that legitimately equip them to function more effectively in one sphere of responsibility than in another.* And the debate heats up when someone suggests that men and women find their deepest joys when they give and receive in unique ways in relationships.

The idea that our distinctively designed bodies reflect distinctively shaped souls triggers more questions.

Am I first a person who functions as a person and who also happens to be man, or am I a male person whose deepest being is somehow distinct from my wife's?

Does my sexuality merely decorate my soul—or define it? When a surgeon completes a sex-change operation on a man, does he produce a *woman* or a *disfigured man,* who for complex reasons feels more at home in a female body?

Is there something uniquely feminine about a woman that makes it more natural for her to *receive* her husband in their everyday relationship, the way she physically receives him in the bedroom? Is there something uniquely masculine about a man that makes it more natural for him to move toward his wife in relationship the way he physically moves toward her in the bedroom?

Is encouraging a little girl to become a mature *person* the same as encouraging her to become a mature *woman?* Are masculine and feminine maturity different?

These are tough questions, the kind that require us eventually to come down on one side or the other. I have landed on the side of those who believe there is an essential difference between men and women—a difference that is properly reflected in unique styles of relating both with their worlds and with one another.

The trouble with taking a position is that I am not entirely comfortable in the company that answering either way requires me to keep. Those who hold there is a difference and imply that the really important thing is for women to know their place think with a soul-smothering rigidity I abhor. Even those who more graciously speak of *roles* for men and women sometimes tend toward a "box-them-in" approach to relationships that limits intimacy.

But those who believe that personhood is more basic to identity than gender and that the differences between men and women have no bearing on how each was designed to relate are moving in directions that I think are dangerous and wrong. If our approach to relationships and responsibilities reflects not only our personality and gifts but also our sexual nature, then eliminating the unique element that each sex brings to their community will distort a good design.

Let me restate the central question of this chapter: Is there something masculine about men and feminine about women that needs to be expressed in meaningfully different ways as they relate to one another for God's design to be most fully realized in this world?

My answer is yes, and I give it with neither qualification that would water it down, nor apology that would betray a weakness of conviction. The question, however, does not lend itself well to a simple answer because it touches on so many issues that deserve careful thought and require wise judgment. Others who answer yes sometimes mean very different things than I do, and I sense a strong kinship with some of the thinking of those who answer no.

My one word answer therefore will not do. It needs explanation. In the remainder of this chapter, I want to discuss my reasons for answering the question as I do and to suggest why some would answer no.

## WHY I ANSWER YES

### Intuitive Reasons

It is interesting to notice that several who believe as I do, that masculinity and femininity describe something important and central about our identity, sometimes appeal to a *natural sense* about the matter.

Elisabeth Elliot, in her foreword to John Piper's book *What's the Difference? Manhood and Womanhood Defined According to the Bible,* concludes her endorsement of the book's traditionalist perspective by saying, "I think his thesis rings true to the manliness or womanliness in each of us."[1] Near the end of the same book, after naming the lack of spiritual leadership by men as a terribly serious sin, Piper writes, "and to the degree that this makes room for women to take more leadership, it is sometimes even endorsed as a virtue. But I believe that *deep down* (emphasis mine) the men—and the women— know better."[2]

Now if the only defense for this viewpoint on masculinity and femininity is intuition, it is a weak one. When the defense is part of a larger rationale that marshals support from both Scripture and experience, then an argument from "internal witness" is entirely legitimate for deepening conviction and for sometimes tipping the scales toward one position over another.

And this is quite as it should be. If God, in fact, did build something called masculinity and femininity into our very natures, then we would expect to feel a "fit" between our experience of ourselves as men or women and an accurate description of what it means to be sexual beings.

However, because we live in a fallen world and because the fall dropped us to a lower plane of existence (we are now "submen" and "subwomen"), a true description of who we are will not ring true to everyone. Those most aware of the ideal that redemption is restoring will affirm true descriptions and retreat uncomfortably from false ones.

This leaves us, of course, in the awkward position of wondering whether our internal ring reflects a clear or distorted vision of the way things should be. Are we mature and therefore perceptive, or is our vision blurred by unrecognized immaturity?

The best we can do is hold our convictions firmly but not rigidly, define maturity carefully as other-centered relating, pursue it by persistently facing our self-centeredness and learning to enjoy God's forgiveness, saturate ourselves in Scripture and prayer, and remain open to whatever image of sexuality emerges within us as we grow more in what it means to love.

It would be wrong, of course, to require that *my* intuitive sense of what feels masculine or feminine guide *your* understanding. But it is legitimate if I permit *my* understanding to be influenced by *my* natural sense about the matter.

And it also seems reasonable to give weight to the intuitive feel of people whose relational maturity we respect. For me, those people are ones who are eager to know how others experience them, who are bothered when their impact is bad and grateful when it is good, and who care as much about relating in love as about proclaiming sound doctrine. Their numbers, I think, are few.

My impression is that their intuition often supports me in believing that men and women are different in ways that matter.

## Experiential Reasons

A second line of support, useful, but no more definitive than intuition, comes from counseling experience. Let me illustrate with two from several hundred possible examples.

The two examples I have selected are a man and a woman, each struggling with homosexual temptation. Sometimes the lack of a deeply felt sense of masculinity or femininity, a problem common to folks struggling with homosexual desires, provides an interesting slant on the characteristics of masculinity and femininity.

A Christian man converted from a homosexual lifestyle told me of his continuing battle with temptation. I probed deeply, wanting to know what he found compelling about homosexual activity. I assumed that this attraction was a counterfeit of the masculine satisfaction he was built to enjoy. His answer, pieced together from several conversations, was revealing.

It really isn't the physical pleasure of sexual release that means the most to me. I enjoy that, of course, but it's sexual pleasure *with a man* that I want. Sometimes I feel an incredible build up of pressure within me. It seems that nothing will relieve it except being with a man in a sexual way. I literally get consumed with my desire.

But it isn't the sex itself that relieves the pressure. Or maybe a better way to put it is that it isn't just sexual pressure that gets relieved. It's deeper than that. When I'm enjoying a personal sense of intimacy with a man, *something partial in me feels completed*. Something I really want to be seems somehow within reach. And this means so much to me that whatever it costs to get, it seems worth it, at least at the time. But later, I don't feel good. I feel like I need to be completed again.

Shortly after that series of conversations, I spoke with another friend, this one a single woman who occasionally experiences lesbian attractions. With tears of desperate confusion and self-disgust, she told me how angry she would sometimes feel when her female roommate (*not* a lesbian lover) went out on a date. I asked her to describe her internal experience more fully.

I know it's crazy and unreasonable, but I feel somehow betrayed when she meets a guy for a date, like she is breaking a bond between us. There's never been anything sexual between us, and I really don't want there to be. It's something deeper than this that I want.

What scares me most is that I'm seeing a pattern. I seem to always attach myself to one special person—usually a woman (somehow they make me feel safer than men), and then I guess I let our relationship mean too much to me, because if they back away at all, I feel jilted.

Reminding myself that she's still my friend whether she dates or not doesn't help very much. I think I want her all to myself—and if not her, then someone. I just can't stand being alone and unwanted.

The man talks of feeling *complete*, the woman of feeling *attached*.

In her intriguing book *In a Different Voice*, Carol Gilligan reports dozens of research studies that suggest similar feelings among men and women in general, not just among those struggling with homosexual temptation.[3]

According to Gilligan, men see themselves as maturing when they can separate themselves as individuals. They tend to value independence and mastery as the route to feeling both complete and able to move confidently through life. Women, on the other hand, seem more concerned with developing close relationships that are held together by an interdependent bonding. Gilligan observes that for men, maturity has more to do with feeling strong within themselves and that for women, maturity depends on the ability to enjoy warm attachments.

If men and women do, in fact, speak "in a different voice," as Gilligan suggests, perhaps it is because they are meaningfully different in their deepest longings and in their approach to relationships and responsibilities. And perhaps phrases like "complete-ness within oneself" and a desire to "enter one's world with impact" versus "attachment to others" and a desire to "enjoy the world of intimate relationships" begin to get at the difference.

## Theological Reasons

Intuition and experience merely suggest directions for thought. Scripture instructs our thinking. If the Bible drives me to a theology that contradicts both intuition and experience, I must handle the tension with a firm commitment to honor biblical instruction above any other source of input. But in the matter of male-female distinctiveness, I have encountered no substantive contradiction between my hunches and observations and my study of Scripture. Let me now present a few theological reasons that have directed my thinking.

I have earlier suggested that the doctrine of the Trinity teaches us two supremely important lessons. First, the most important thing we do with our lives is to enter and develop relationship, first with God, then with others. Nothing matters more in life, nothing is more meaningful to life, than the quality of our relationships with God and with others. Our relationship with ourselves (self-image, sense of purpose, and so on) is good only to the degree that our relationship with God and with others is as it should be. That's the first lesson we learn from knowing that God is one and yet a trinity of Persons whose very existence is an eternal relationship.

The second lesson we learn from the Trinity is this: A good relationship is one in which each person uses his or her resources primarily to promote the other's well being and not his or her own, regardless of the cost. Martin Luther put it even more strongly when he wrote: "To love is not to wish good for another person, it is to bear another's burden; that is, to bear what is painful to you and which you do not bear willingly."[4] (I presume *willingly* here means something like *naturally*.) When we say that God is love, we mean that the three Persons of the Godhead always relate with perfect other-centered energy toward one another and toward their creatures. Good relating is therefore other-centered relating.

But there is a third lesson: Relationships have a nonreversible order. The three members of the Trinity have divided up the responsibilities of creation, redemption, and administration among themselves in an orderly, nonexchangeable but often overlapping fashion. Their purposes are one and their value to these purposes equal, but their responsibilities are, to an important degree, distinguishable.

For example, the Son, according to John 1:1 – 3, assumed responsibility for creation. But in the plan of redemption, he submitted himself to the Father in a way that the Father did not submit himself to the Son. Although the oneness of relationship involved each submitting to the other with pure other-centeredness, the Son submitted to the Father in a way that cannot be turned around, a "one-way" submission that carries with it no hint of inferiority in the one who submits. The Son's submission reflects a chosen course of action according to a purposeful design.

It is this idea of nonreversible order in relationships, the third lesson of the trinity, that I now want to explore briefly because it provides good reason to expect that marriage, the central relationship among God's creatures, should exhibit a similar order of *different but equal responsibilities*.

It should be noted, lest we place an unfair weight on this analogy, that there is an obvious distinction within the trinity and human relationships: Each member of the trinity is perfectly other-centered; no member of a human relationship can make the same claim. Our Lord did not need to reckon with sinfulness in his Father or rebellion in himself as he submitted to the Father's plan. The Father had no need to worry if his motives in directing his Son's activity were unloving. But in human relationships, the stain of self-centeredness is a reality that always must be taken into account.

God clearly loves order (1 Cor. 14:33, 40). He not only lives according to an intrinsic order, he also stamps an order onto everything he creates. God is no distant king who sets things in motion and then retreats from involvement. He is creator and *sustainer* of the universe. It is God, not nature, who presides as the sun rises over the horizon every morning at a predictable time. God is not bored by regularity, he rather delights in creative expression within fixed boundaries.

The order God stamped into creation extends into his creation of man and woman. Consider a few indications of that order.

1. God created Adam first, then Eve (1 Cor. 11:8, 9). This orderly plan made their relationship suitable for representing the nonreversible order that would later mark the relationship between Christ and his church (Eph. 5:21–33).

2. God declared that Adam's existence without

Eve was not good. Why? Was the reason more than just the absence of merely human companionship? Was there something uniquely *male* about Adam's humanness that was designed to enjoy relationship with a being that was equally human but distinctly *female*? And was there something about maleness that could function together with femaleness in exercising dominion in this world?

After God declared that it was not good for the man to be alone and before he created Eve, God arranged for Adam to name the animals. I wonder why God gave this task to Adam right before he introduced him to Eve. We are told (Gen. 2:20) that Adam did not find a suitable companion among all the animals. Was he looking for one? Did *he* come to realize through this experience that something was missing?

Spending hours (days? weeks? months?) naming the animals must have aroused in Adam an unclear but still strong sense that something within him yearned to reach out but that there was nothing there to properly receive his touch. It was *then* that God put him to sleep.

When he woke up and for the first time saw a woman, someone wonderfully different from the animals and wonderfully like him, but uniquely shaped to receive his touch, he shouted, "Now I am complete! Whatever within me that was partial is now whole!"

Eve was then joined to Adam *by the strength of his commitment to her* (Gen. 2:23–25), and in their union she felt the joys of nonmanipulative, mutually giving attachment.

3. After they both had sinned, Adam and Eve covered themselves and hid. Adam and Eve sensed

that something about them was now unaccept-
able! — a good design was corrupted. But exactly
what was ugly about them? What did their disobe-
dience corrupt?

Perhaps Adam's commitment *as a man* to his
woman was perverted into a rejection of God's
authority. Perhaps Eve's enjoyment *as a woman* of
her man was seen as less than the potential enjoyment of something forbidden. In other words,
Adam shifted his allegiance away from God to
Eve, and Eve shifted her allegiance away from
God and his design for her to the giver of the forbidden fruit.

Thus, Adam and Eve's standing naked before
God exposed something ugly about their sexual
identity as man and woman. Their sinfulness
extended into the deepest parts of their beings. If
at core they are male and female, persons with
distinctive sexual identities, then their masculinity and femininity were deeply involved in the
corruption.

4. When God confronted the hiding pair, he
spoke *first* to Adam. Why? A random choice? Or
did God view Adam's responsibility differently
(not more or less severely) because he was a *man*?

Paul speaks of Adam, not Eve, as the one
through whom sin entered the world, even though
Eve sinned first and both sinned as individuals.
And he refers to Christ as the last Adam (1 Cor.
15:22, 45). Is there not some distinction here
between man and woman that goes beyond the
physical?

5. God's judgment of Eve was on both her
uniquely feminine capacity to give birth and her
relationship with Adam. In other words, her

*physical attachment* to Adam would lead to moments of excruciating pain (in childbirth) and her *personal attachment* would involve heartache and battle.

Adam's judgment was different. God required him to endure previously unknown difficulties as he sought to subdue his world. He would now have to work in a hostile environment where he would often fail and to live with a woman who would now be more concerned with her own needs than with his. He lost the sense of *completion* that comes from *powerfully subduing his world* and meaningfully touching a woman *who would, as a priority, value his work and enjoy his involvement.*

I conclude that there is an order to male-female relationships that is nonreversible because it reflects the differences God built into us. Although I will more carefully describe masculinity and femininity in the next chapter, perhaps I can draw from the order of creation some beginning thoughts about maleness and femaleness.

Maleness has something to do with the sense of completion that a man gets from strongly moving into his world with an enjoyed commitment (at least in potential) to a female companion. Single men can live with an awareness of their capacity to move toward a woman and a willingness to do so as circumstances permit. They therefore can fully experience themselves as men.

Femaleness may include a capacity for bonding to a man to encourage him with the support of one who values and respects him, who invites him into relationship with her, and who enjoys being enjoyed by him.* This capacity may not always have opportunity for expression but it is always there in a woman's nature.

The joys of maleness and femaleness are meaningfully available to all men and women who are growing in other-centeredness. Marriage, however, grants a unique opportunity for enjoying certain forms of intimacy that singleness does not provide, including sexual relations and a lifelong commitment of companionship.

Are there differences between men and women that are knowable and deep enough to justify a distinct approach to relating within the home and church? I've answered yes but many folks answer no.

## WHY MANY ANSWER NO

Much of the debate over the place of women in the church and home has centered on a study of the so-called "problem passages" (1 Cor. 11:3—16; Gal. 3:28; Eph. 5:21—33; Col. 3:18, 19; 1 Tim. 2:8—15; 3:1—13; Titus 2:1—5). The response one gives to any question the Bible addresses, including the one with which we are now concerned, must, of course, be rooted in an effort to understand the relevant passages. Evangelicals who answer no to the question I am now discussing (as well as those who answer yes) offer their interpretation of the Bible as reason for their convictions.

---

*The word *enjoyed* could be heard to mean "enjoyed" as an object. I intend to use the word to mean "to delight in" as in a distinctly different creation of God.

And rightly so. Each of us must study the difficult passages as best we can, valuing the insights and knowledge of other students, and reach our understanding of what the Bible teaches.

In this section, however, I want to look at two reasons why some believe that masculinity and femininity are either not deeply different or are indefinably different, two reasons that do not depend on an understanding of *specific* biblical texts.

## Intuitive Reasons

Many men and women simply do not feel an intuitive agreement with the theory of substantial differences. Their internal experiences support a view that holds to no such differences. If the "substantial difference" theory is correct, shouldn't all (or at least most) people experience the differences within themselves?

My response is, "Not necessarily." Here's why. One of the great marks of our fallen humanness is our ability to escape from personal pain by dulling the nerve endings of our souls. Much as starving people can sometimes relieve their agony by convincing themselves they are really not hungry, so lonely people can deny to themselves how badly they long for companionship.

Now, if it is true that each of us is at core either masculine or feminine, if every child is either a little boy or a little girl in ways that extend deeply into their souls, then the hurt provoked by imperfect love, whether an insensitive comment or cruel rejection, will be experienced as an assault on our existence as male or female, not merely as a threat to a neutral sense of personhood.

When we hurt, nothing matters more than finding relief. Because we are fallen, we do not naturally turn to God for protection and love. We want to find some way that *we control* to restore a sense of personal well-being.

A common solution to the problem of inescapable pain in our masculine and feminine souls is to anesthetize the part of our being that has been most deeply hurt. We therefore cut off from our own awareness what is most thoroughly male or female about us. By ceasing to exist as a man or woman and reducing ourselves to the safer existence of neutered personhood, we are able to face life as intact persons less threatened and more confident. We thereby minimize the fullness of our existence as hurting, vulnerable men and women who cannot function without God.

When we disown the part of ourselves that is most uniquely masculine or feminine, we develop a certain toughness that, although false and repelling, feels good and reflects itself in comments like these:

> I really don't care if people enjoy me.
>
> So what if no one likes me. I'm good at what I do, and people respect me for it.
>
> I just don't want to face how my husband might really feel about me so I just won't ask or think about it anymore. I'll do what I enjoy so I can feel good about myself.
>
> I've learned one thing about people. You can be polite and kind but you can't let them get an advantage over you.
>
> Have I ever made anyone really happy? Dunno! Never thought about it. Well, maybe I'll go eat something.

By cutting the nerves to the deepest part of our sexual selves, we lose much of what we were meant to be to each other as masculine men and feminine women. We settle for being mere persons rather than living up to our manhood and womanhood. We prefer to enjoy the safe assertiveness of a neutered soul than the risky involvement required of men and women.

When we put into passion-filled words what it means to be deeply alive as men and women, those who are defensively determined to remain out of touch with their core sexuality will feel resentful. No bells will ring in their souls. They will therefore honestly report, within the limits of their awareness, that the words do not fit what they know of themselves.

This may not explain why many don't feel a distinct masculinity or femininity within themselves, but I argue that it *could*.

### Theological Reasons

The Bible never defines masculinity or femininity. Perhaps its silence suggests that there really is no such thing. Or, if there is, maybe we are to enjoy it as a mystery and get on with the holy living to which men and women are equally called. The need to define a transcultural understanding of maleness and femaleness may be a trap that will only confuse us and detract from living as Christian people.

When a Christian father wants to teach his son what it means to be a man, what should he say? Some fathers might describe certain responsibilities they believe the Bible assigns more to men than to women, such as providing for a family, nourishing and cherishing one's wife, and assuming the burden of spiritual leadership in the home. They then might teach their sons that masculinity is whatever it takes to do these things well.

Others would respond that the Bible nowhere directly addresses the father's concern. The Bible does say, however, a great deal about the kind of *person* the boy should become, including a few attributes our culture often regards as feminine, such as gentleness and sensitivity. Masculinity is therefore not something to work at developing. Rather, to whatever degree it exists as a distinguishing characteristic, it will take care of itself as the boy pursues the common virtues.

The silence of Scripture on any subject, including this one, must be reckoned with as we develop our ideas. Things would be so much simpler if God had included a passage somewhere that began, "Let me now tell you exactly what it means to be masculine and feminine." Even then, I suppose, we would manage to spot an ambiguity in language or hypothesize about the cultural context in order to make the passage say what we would prefer it to say.

There is, of course, no such passage.

But I wonder if the biblical silence is *less* an indication that there are no sexual distinctives that deserve emphasis and *more* a safeguard against erecting a strict legalistic code of conduct for each sex to follow, the kind of code that traditionalism sometimes develops.

And perhaps the Scriptures are not as silent on the subject as we think. Could it be that the existence of a distinctive sexuality, like the existence of God as Trinity, is an *assumed* truth?

It is true that biblical exhortations are generally addressed to men and women together, but there are notable exceptions: "Wives, submit to your husbands, as is fitting in the Lord. Husbands, love your wives and do not be harsh with them" (Col. 3:18, 19). However we interpret the instructions, the one to wives is different from the one to husbands. If differences in sexual nature are assumed in the Bible, then perhaps even casual comments (if any verse of Scripture can be called "casual") such as, "Be strong and show yourself as a man" (1 Kings 2:2)* may have something to teach us about manhood and womanhood.

## TWO GUIDELINES

I suggest that we observe at least two guidelines in thinking through the difficult subject of sexual differences. *First, we must insist on a relational understanding of what it means to be masculine and feminine,* an understanding that highlights what it is we give to each other rather than merely detailing sexually determined roles and responsibilities.

Manhood and womanhood cannot be reduced to a confining set of duties that must be obeyed or to a list of characteristics that ought to be developed. Thinking of male and female *roles* more than manhood and womanhood encourages us to miss the point that God's instructions are always rooted in the high value he places on relationship. Doing

---

*Interestingly, these are the words of a father to a son, in this case a dying father, David, to the next king of Israel, Solomon.

what he commands will always involve relating as we should.

Therefore I would rather think more about richly relating to one another than pinning down an exact definition of sexuality that we must express in our behavior. The sexual distinctiveness built into us by God will reliably and truly emerge only as we relate with other-centered energy. Whatever develops in any other context is counterfeit.

However, I do believe something meaningful and important can be known about maleness and femaleness. Although there is little hope of ever defining our differences with precision, still our sexuality is more than a completely unknowable mystery to be enjoyed.

My second guideline, therefore, is this: *We should seek to better understand the meaning of masculinity and femininity by studying the nature of the trinity, the creation and the fall of Adam and Eve, and the differing responsibilities that the Bible assigns to men and women.*

In the next chapter, I try to follow these guidelines as I respond to the question, What is masculinity and femininity?

# *Nine*

## Masculinity and Femininity

*Our sexuality penetrates to the deepest metaphysical ground of our personality. As a result, the physical differences between the man and the woman are a parable of the psychical and spiritual differences of a more ultimate nature.*

EMIL BRUNNER

*Any attempt to pinpoint differences between men and* women, especially if these differences become grounds for arguing that the sexes have differing spheres of responsibility in home and church, is likely to create more critics and skeptics than friends. The attempt itself puts us on guard. It makes us tense. A discussion of our sexual distinctiveness touches something deeply personal within us.

This, of course, might be expected if the differences run deep and if our identity as persons is inescapably wrapped up in our manhood or womanhood. It is precisely because I believe that sexual differences do run deep and that understanding them is important that I decided to write this book.

Let me highlight two important matters that are at stake in the discussion: *the design of God in creation* and *the power and joy of his people who are to live by this design.*

I see so many men, like Mike in chapter 7, who haven't the foggiest idea of what they could do to help their wives feel meaningfully loved. Every relationship, of course, runs into times of conflict when neither party knows what is best to do. But husbands too often handle their confusion by retreating from the kind of strong and sensitive involvement that might encourage their wives to internally relax. Instead, they assert an authority that they hope will restore at least some measure of stability to their home.

Many husbands pervert Paul's teaching on headship into a warrant for requiring their wives to always agree with them and to service their every need. Others, attempting to correct this mistake, have renounced any distinctive masculine form of loving their wives and have watched their marriage shift from a cold regime with a leader and a follower into a business arrangement marked more by efficiency than intimate passion.

And countless wives, like Debby, respond to the confusion *either* by submitting themselves into the status of a kept woman or a domestic servant, losing all sense of personal dignity, *or* by liberating themselves into a larger world where they enjoy the respect they deserve while silently crying for the love they want.

It could be different. When husbands are masculine, wives tend to go "off duty." They feel relieved of the relentless pressure to make things go as they should. They relax in the strength of an advocate that frees them to more easily realize the other-centered joy of their womanhood. When wives are feminine, husbands gain confidence in handling responsibilities, and are drawn to warmly enjoy and profoundly respect the woman whose involvement with them means more to their hearts than the most coveted honor or achievement could ever mean. They feel strengthened in deep parts of their being where nothing but femininity can touch.

The possibilities for marital intimacy should neither be overstated, nor understated. No marriage will ever be entirely free of inexcusable selfishness. But there can be tastes, sometimes lingering ones, of an exquisite joy that makes us long to conform more fully to our Creator's design. And as we do so, as we become more other-centered in our sexuality, those tastes may come more frequently and linger a little longer, enabling us to maintain a fairly steady level of mutually enjoyed intimacy.

The taste of good relationship is sweet, and it is enjoyed in regions of our being that nothing else can enter. I experience a distinctly pleasurable rush of emotion when an unexpected sum of money comes my way, but the enjoyment of closeness with another human being is on an entirely different plane. The relational experience is quieter and at the same time far more stirring, something like the difference between the blaring noise of a rock concert and the powerful and majestic sound of a mighty waterfall. One stimulates frantic excitement (and, in me, at least, a headache), the other stirs rich movement. Only the fool prefers shallow excitement over movement in deep parts of the soul. Relationship matters as nothing else does.

And if there is something masculine about a man and feminine about a woman that spouses can *uniquely* enjoy, then thinking about what these terms mean seems worth the effort.

I offer my ideas as unfinished, nondogmatic convictions, but still as *convictions* which, because they have persuaded and helped me, will, I hope, persuade and help you.

One conviction about how men and women relate stands out more than the others. Many people would be helped to relate in more godly fashion, and there would be less frustrating confusion and pushy debate if we kept in mind this central principle: A person's true sexuality emerges only as he or she relates morally to others.

## RELATING MORALLY

It is interesting to notice that when we reject his authority over our lives, God does not protect us from sexual perversion.[1] In the first chapter of Romans, Paul traces the development of unnatural sexual urges from refusal to honor God (vv. 21−23).

Because God "gave them over" to what he never intended, sexual desires unique to each gender were corrupted, urges that Paul labels "unnatural" developed in men and women. Paul describes the emergence of perverted lust as one part of a definite sequence of events:

*First,* the people reject God as worthy of worship and praise (v. 21).

*Second,* they exchange God for images of themselves, and they depend on resources within themselves to gain and preserve life (v. 25).

*Third,* they lose discernment (vv. 21, 22). Because we were designed to live in relationship, this loss of discernment primarily involves a wrong understanding of how to get along with one another.

*Fourth,* even though they are dreadfully wrong, they are convinced they are right (vv. 22—23).

*Fifth,* the first clear evidence that they are wrong is the breakdown of relationship between the sexes (vv. 24—27). God's design for sexual relating becomes *trivialized* into mere erotic passion and *corrupted* into impurity and perversion.

*Sixth,* people become hardened in their rebellious understanding of life. Beginning with the corruption of their sexual natures, they extend their wickedness by defiling all their relationships at every level (vv. 18—31).

*Seventh,* they live in arrogant defiance of God's promised judgment and contemptuously take pleasure in welcoming others into their wicked style of living.

Two parts of this disastrous sequence must be underscored. *First,* self-centeredness kicks the entire process into motion. The root sin is arrogant conceit that honors our welfare as supremely important and that stubbornly depends on our own resources to provide for our souls.

*Second,* it is important to see that God's first act

of judgment led to the misuse and corruption of our sexual natures. Self-centeredness is the root problem, with sexual confusion its first consequence. A failure to humble ourselves before God by repenting of our commitment to look after our own welfare can harden us in a wrong understanding of how to live in this world as men and women. It can distort our sexuality so that legitimate male and female desires are overwhelmed by impure and perverted lusts.

Understanding masculinity and femininity begins with learning what another person needs with the intent of supplying that need if we can. It does not begin by trying to understand ourselves.

When we emphasize providing others with what they need rather than on figuring out who we are, what is most valuable, real, and substantial about us will surface. Giving out of compassion for recognized human need stirs us to boldly give the very best we have.[2]

*True masculinity and femininity emerge and develop only in the midst of other-centered relating.*

The more a man understands a woman and is controlled by a Spirit-prompted other-centered commitment to bless her, the more "masculine" he becomes. And he will become more masculine in an unself-conscious fashion. Ask this man to define masculinity, and he will need to think a while before answering.

In exactly the same way, the more a woman understands a man and is preoccupied with doing all she can for him, the more "feminine" she naturally becomes. We will neither understand nor enjoy our sexual natures until we take seriously our responsibility to use our distinct natures to serve others.

I therefore offer a beginning definition of masculinity and femininity: Masculinity and femininity are whatever comes out of a man and a woman as they do not try to excuse their self-centeredness, but repent whenever they spot it, and as they learn to relate to others as Christ does with an increasingly passionate concern for their well-being. More can be said about our sexual identities, but nothing more important.

If your marriage is troubled, my counsel is not to figure out what it means to be a man or woman, then try hard to measure up to your definition, nor to fit into whatever *role* may be implied by your definition. Nor is my counsel to determine who you are as a person, whether male or female, with your own set of interests, talents, and resources, and then learn to more fully *express* whatever you discover, committing yourself to removing whatever obstacles you encounter.

My counsel is rather to look hard at your spouse, to identify *his* or *her* hurts and wounds and frustrations, and then to do whatever is within your power to help. The obstacles you need to remove are those that interfere with your progress toward other-centeredness, not with self-expression.

Following this simply stated bit of advice will bring you into the legitimate and wholesome enjoyment of your true self, whether you are male or female.

Learning to be other-centered then is the foundation for masculine and feminine relating. Scripture does more, however, than lay the foundation. It also provides a basis for thinking more specifically about what it means to be a man or woman.

Drawing from the *lessons of the Trinity,* the *biblical account of creation and the fall,* and the *separate responsibilities assigned to men and women,* I now want to explore the nature of our sexuality in order to help us better understand how we can relate with an other-centeredness that bears the mark of our manhood or womanhood.

## THE NATURE OF MASCULINITY

When does a man feel most like a man? What makes him glad that he is a man, grateful to be alive because of the unique joys of masculinity?

Because God created us *for* relationship, because we find our reason to exist *in* relationship, and because life's deepest joys come to us *through* relationship, masculinity is most richly expressed in relationships. It is in relationship that a man achieves a satisfying sense of completion. But what is this thing we so easily refer to as "masculinity"?

Two elements are involved: *a quiet confidence* as a man moves purposefully through life, aware that what he has to give makes a good difference and *a tender sensitivity to others* that makes him willing to decisively and sacrificially involve himself with another. Consider them both.

Although God delegated authority over the earth to both the man and woman, it is difficult to escape the impression that God intended the *man* to move into the world in a way that differed from his intention for the woman. After the fall, God's judgment on Adam introduced difficulties that affected him as he *worked in the world*. The judgment was not that he had to work, but rather that his work would not go smoothly.

Eve's judgment, on the other hand, centered on *her relationship with the man*, both as the one who would bear the couple's children and in her efforts to enjoy companionship with him (see Gen. 3:16—19).

God's judgments on both the man and the woman were neither petulant nor uncaring. God's intent was to discourage Adam and Eve (and their descendants) from thinking that their lives could ever work without him and to help them realize that the full realization of joy awaits a new heaven and earth. He wanted to hedge them in, to surface a despair that would drive them back to himself.

We can assume therefore that when he judged the man and the woman, God introduced problems into the very core of their existence. For Adam, that meant struggles as *he moved into his world*. For Eve, that meant pain as *she related to Adam*.

Paul's instruction that older women should teach younger women to be "busy at home" (Titus 2:5) further suggests that the spheres of a man's and woman's responsibilities, though overlapping considerably, are in some measure distinguishable.

This thought is easily abused. No executive or businessman may use this passage to justify working long and hard at his office and letting his wife handle things at home. Nor can a pastor or missionary assume that his call to ministry frees him to do "God's business" while his wife raises the children.

God specifically warns husbands not to be so involved outside the family that they neglect responsibilities at home (1 Tim. 3:4; 1 Peter 3:7). And he makes it clear that a husband's responsibility within his home extends far beyond material provision. God directly commands the husband to love his wife according to the example of one who sacrificed all, including his position, to remove obstacles to relationship that *his bride had created* and to thereby introduce her to an intimacy they could both enjoy (Eph. 5:21—33).

Directions to the husband specifically include nourishing his wife (providing for her needs) and cherishing (tenderly handling) her according to a thought-through understanding of her sensitivities (Eph. 5:29; 1 Peter 3:7), whether it is in the tender, intimate life-generating physical relationship or in the confidence with which he approaches decisions in life. Most men will, of course, go through troublesome times of uncertainty, but as long as there is a confidence beneath the turmoil that things will sort themselves out, the sense of masculinity continues to be felt.

A woman will not, however, enjoy the company, at least not for long, of a supremely confident man who never struggles with self-doubt, whose confidence is a swaggering belief in his ability to reach self-serving goals. The successful, talented, attractive man who doesn't know how to expose his weaknesses and sensitively explore his wife's feelings will not win her appreciation. Neither macho nor wimpy describes a man.

A man is "manly" when he moves through life

with a purposeful and confident involvement, when he follows a direction that he values for reasons that are bigger than himself. If that direction reflects the purposes of God, then his style of relating will not be self-consumed, driven, or pushy; it will rather reflect a growing sensitivity to others and an unhurried involvement with them that can be neither manipulated nor stopped. Indications that he is pulling appreciation or applause or confirmation from others to feed either an oversized or a starving ego will lessen the enjoyable impact of his masculinity on both himself and others.

When a man's purposes are godly, that is, when he is ambitious for God's glory and concerned with other-centered relating, he will experience a stability that anchors him through emotional ups and downs (which he will therefore be unafraid to experience) and a noble desire for tender, caring, intimate involvement with people, primarily his wife. In this involvement his wife will feel secure, conscious that she is more enjoyed and valued than his greatest achievements.

Masculinity is not so much a matter of what a man does, but that *he does it* and that he does it *for certain reasons*. Little things, for example, like rubbing your wife's neck when it is sore, will be felt as "masculine" even though another man or a woman could provide the same service for your wife, and perhaps more competently. It is the demonstrated and eager sensitivity to another's need that feels masculine to both partners when a husband rubs his wife's sore neck.

A masculine man knows, with a sense of gratitude rather than pride, that there will be impact for good as he moves into his world and that what he gives is most worthy of respect when it touches the longings of his wife's heart. Masculinity disposes a man to move decisively and compassionately into his world and toward family and friends with a joyful confidence that he can promote good purposes.

When the substance within him that defines his male identity is moving with other-centered energy, a man feels a completion and wholeness that makes selfish achievement and immoral pleasures less appealing. Nothing brings a man quite the same level of masculine pleasure as touching his wife in a way that brings her joy and confidence as a woman and that frees her to enjoy all that she is and can become.

Masculinity, I suggest, might therefore be thought of as *the satisfying awareness of the substance God has placed within a man's being that can make an enduring contribution to God's purposes in this world, and will be deeply valued by others, especially his wife, as a reliable source of wise, sensitive, compassionate, and decisive involvement.*

## THE NATURE OF FEMININITY

Womanhood must never be defined in a frivolous way that makes it necessarily "unfeminine" to be fully competent and highly respected as a physician, corporate executive, or biblical scholar. Nor should femininity be somehow essentially connected to cooking, sensual clothing, or a sweet, subservient demeanor. Womanhood, like manhood, has more to do with a woman's attitude toward herself and others as she involves herself in relationships.

A godly woman is more interested in giving whatever she has to meet someone's need than in developing her talents, and she is aware that her uniquely feminine contribution depends more than anything else on matters within her heart that affect her style of relating.

I have suggested that a man experiences himself as masculine when he knows that his very substance is a gift from God moving confidently in the lives of others. A woman feels most uniquely feminine when she enjoys her capacity to strengthen relationships and to encourage others by inviting them to enjoy the blessings of relationship.

A woman is less centrally focused on *achievement* as a means for feeling complete (although a graduating female medical student may be just as happy to finish school as a graduating male). More, she tends to value giving something of herself to nourish relationships and deepen attachments. Her focus is less on *going into the world* and more on *entering a relational network*.

Researcher Carol Gilligan, in arguing her central thesis that women approach life differently than men, reported on a series of interviews with highly successful professional women:

> In response to the request to describe themselves, all of the women describe a relationship, depicting their identity in the connection of future mother, present wife, adopted child, or past lover. These highly successful women do not mention their academic and professional

distinctions in the context of describing themselves. If anything, they regard their professional activities as jeopardizing their own sense of themselves. . . . Identity is defined in the context of relationship.[3]

She goes on to say that men see themselves more as separate individuals, achieving something, than as persons whose identity is found in relational attachments. "Instead of attachment, individual achievement rivets the male imagination."[4]

The ideas of *separateness* and *achievement* and *entering* seem more rooted in the masculine nature while *involvement* and *attachment* and *invitation* belong more clearly to feminine identity.

I recently received a letter from a husband and wife who wrote to tell me about how they were growing and maturing. The different emphasis in each of their comments illustrates my point. In part of her letter, the woman wrote:

> I see two major things now that are being built upon that good foundation [past growth]: The first is that I am able to experience and own my depravity in wonderful, painful ways that are causing true repentance and brokenness. Though the reality of my own wretchedness is excruciating, I'm often somehow aware *in* the pain of a thrill that I am where I am. The second is a great desire *to stand with my arms outstretched, beckoning others to life* and because I've learned and experienced truth and reality I can say with confidence, "Come on friends, come away from death, choose life!" What a privilege—what a high calling (emphasis mine).

Her husband, in the same letter, expressed himself differently, focusing more on his ministry:

> I believe that *we are on the cutting edge and are presenting the gospel* in a profoundly relevant way. I write this with humility and thankfulness as I see a quietly powerful revolution happening in the lives of people as they turn from useless idols to pursue the living God. All of this is precious to me* (emphasis mine).

The difference is noteworthy. The woman sees herself as *inviting others* to taste the Lord through her. The man sees himself as *moving toward others* with powerful impact. I do not think it stretches things too far to regard *physical* sexuality as a wonderful picture of *personal* sexuality: men feel complete as they strongly enter; women feel enjoyed as they warmly invite.

Femininity, at its core, might therefore be thought of as the secure awareness of the substance God has placed within a woman's being that enables her to confidently and warmly invite others into relationship with God and with herself, knowing that there is something in each relationship to be wonderfully enjoyed.

---

*In this personal communication from friends, it is worthwhile to note that the wife experienced her husband as a man because of his strong involvement with his work and his vulnerable participation in her life. She said, "You would want to worship if you could see him now. It's as if the wonderful qualities God placed within him are being freed and he's just blossoming as a human being, as a man. We're not afraid of each other anymore, so there's wonderful freedom to be mirrors for each other and therefore to be active participants in the growth of each other's soul."

These thoughts about masculinity and femininity are neither precise enough to qualify as definitions nor complete enough to bear direct implications for all the questions about male-female relationships. They do, however, say enough to carry the discussion further.

# *Ten*

## Unique Ways to Freely Love

*Sacrificial love is . . . a form of love which transcends the limits of love. It is a form of love which cannot be embodied in any moral code.*

REINHOLD NIEBUHR

*In obedience man adheres to the Decalogue, and in freedom man creates new decalogues.*

MARTIN LUTHER

*With a few thoughts about masculinity and femininity in* place, we can now answer the questions that we asked in chapter 7 about Mike and Debby. Remember that Mike had discovered marijuana in their son Todd's car. Debby doesn't know. Should Mike tell her?

Because Debby handles the family finances, she knows how desperate their money problems are. But whenever she brings up the topic, Mike becomes upset. Should she tell him how bad the situation really is or should she suffer in silence?

If couples are to not only survive the inevitable hardships of life, but enjoy one another, then each partner needs to know what he or she can give to the other that will bond them together. If Mike and Debby are committed to putting each other first—

to other-centered relating—then we can ask: What does Mike have *as a man* that Debby, *as a woman*, longs to receive? And what does Debby have *as a woman* that Mike, *as a man*, longs to receive?

Is there a difference between men and women that can be enjoyed, a difference in what they can give and what they want to receive? If there is a parallel between *physically* relating and *personally* relating as I suggested in the last chapter, then perhaps women want a strong advocate who frees them to enjoy the uniqueness of their femininity. And perhaps men want to move into their worlds compassionately and confidently and to be deeply valued by their wives. If so, the fit is perfect.

If Mike were warmly and confidently eager to provide tender advocacy for Debby ("Because I'm *for* you, I want to know what you desire and to do all that I can to satisfy those desires"), then Debby would be able to sense his interest in her well-being. Whether or not he shares the bad news of Todd's suspected drug abuse with Debby isn't the central point. What matters is the energy behind whatever decision he makes.

So many times, husbands share hard news with an angry spirit: "This is your fault! If you wouldn't have been so easy on our son, he would have turned out better." Or, if they choose to keep bad news to themselves, they often do so in a noble mood of burden-bearing that communicates disdain for their wives.

We must get it out of our heads that there is only one right course of action to take in every situation. Before we have the wisdom to decide what to do, we must be committed to other-centeredness and sensitive to what such relating requires of us.

It would be impossible to write a husband's manual with clear instructions about when to share what in all situations.

Living biblically in relationship requires courage to make risky decisions that come out of hearts wanting above all else to give. A mere willingness to do whatever conforms to a moral code will not move our relationships toward intimacy.

If Mike is both other-centered and aware of his wife's longing for the tender strength that defines his manhood, then Debby will feel nourished and cherished in her deepest being, whether or not he tells her about Todd's drug problems.

Now how about Debby? What can she give to Mike?

Men are different from women. They feel meaningfully encouraged not by a strong advocate who moves toward them but rather by a woman who appreciatively and respectfully accepts their efforts to handle the responsibilities of life.

A good friend recently told me about the time he and his wife were taking a walk in the woods. He was carrying their infant daughter in a backpack. As he approached a steep hill, his wife, walking a few feet behind, called out, "Be careful!"

He instantly felt irritated. Why? As we talked it through, it became clear that he interpreted her warning to mean something like this: "I'm not sure I can trust you to take care of our daughter. You tend to be so irresponsible at times. If I didn't remind you to be careful, the way a mother would caution a reckless boy, you might do something really stupid." He heard in her words a thorough lack of concern for his sense of adequacy as a man.

Whether or not he heard correctly, his responsibility to his wife is to satisfy her longing for an advocate in an uncertain world. He might therefore warmly reassure her of his intention to take special care of the daughter that means so much to her mother's heart. Snapping at his wife in disgust would be inexcusably self-centered.

But think more about the wife. Her responsibility is to surround her husband with appreciative warmth. If she were sensitive to his longing for respect, then even an admonition to be careful could be given without a demeaning bite.

So, too, with Debby. Mike longs to feel more confident in his ability to provide a good living for his family and to make a pleasurable impact on Debby. If Debby were aware of her capacity to feel richly touched by her husband and of his desire to pleasurably touch her, then she could invite him into deeper relationship by clearly expressing her pleasure in being his wife.

This sort of invitation is risky. It places Debby in a vulnerable position where Mike could more deeply hurt her if he chooses. But this invitation also has the power to reassure Mike that he can make a meaningful difference in Debby's life, regardless of his income. And if the tone in her voice and the look in her eye reflects a respectful, appreciative concern to encourage Mike's sense of manhood, then Mike may feel substantially less threatened by an open discussion about money problems.

If men were designed to enter their worlds with a humble but confident intention to do good and if women were designed to invite people into their worlds to experience the joys of relationships, then perhaps we have a basis for thinking through how men and women can enjoy each other's differences. And perhaps the principles of headship and submission can be understood not merely as roles to fit into, but as opportunities to enjoy the differences.

Headship and submission present us with the chance to satisfy the unique desires of our mates by giving what is distinctively ours to give.


## THREE ILLUSTRATIONS

Look at the following typical marital conflicts and how they could be resolved if the participants understood headship and submission as other-centered activity that reflects the differences between men and women.

### Marriage #1

I think our family should relocate. My wife wants to stay put so that the kids can be close to their grandparents. But a move could be really important to my career; and besides, we already live almost 300 miles from the nearest grandparents. Where I want to move is more than twice that far away but that just means a longer plane ride. And with a better job, I could afford it. But she gets really emotional when I even mention the idea of moving. I'm not sure what to do.

### Marriage #2

It seems like such a small thing, but it happens all the time so maybe it's important. Last night my husband and I were exhausted. We each had really bad days and all we wanted to do was relax in front of the TV. Well, he settled into the big old recliner he likes so much, and I curled up on the couch with a quilt over me.

As soon as we both were settled and comfortable, the phone rang. Neither of us moved. After about three rings, my husband said in his most tired voice, "Honey, could you get it?"

Well, I immediately felt irritated. I *knew* he was going to ask *me* to get up. I was tired, too, and I feel like I'm always the one who waits on him, like he thinks that's my role or something. So I said, "I just got comfortable. I wish you'd get it this time."

Well, you would have thought I asked him to run to the store at midnight. He stared at me for a second with utter disgust, then he got up. But by the time he reached the phone, it had stopped ringing. We barely said a word to each other the rest of the evening. Was I wrong? Am I supposed to get the phone just because he tells me to?

## Marriage #3

My wife gets upset over the smallest things, and I mean *really* upset. She cries and even screams over nothing. Usually, she just gets cold toward me and mopes around for a couple hours, sometimes a few days. And it's usually some dumb little thing that sets her off, like if I forget to mail a letter she gives me when I go to work. I just don't know why she gets so mad.

When I try to talk reasonably about whatever got her going, or even apologize, she never listens. She just gets more emotional and irrational and says really ugly things about me. A couple months ago, when she was super upset, she threatened to divorce me.

I'm stumped. Sometimes I try to be extra nice and helpful, or I tease her about something. I even surprised her with an expensive gift I couldn't afford a while ago. That helped a little.

But other times—and it's happening more often—I get so mad I walk out of the house and slam the door. When I come back an hour or two later, she is usually in a little softer mood. Maybe I ought to get mad more often. Does she just want me to be tougher?

We have thought about self-centeredness, repentance, forgiveness, humility, and differences between men and women. Now it's time to wonder what this all means in an actual marriage relationship.

What does it mean that "the husband is the head of the wife" and that wives are told to "submit to [their] husbands" (Eph. 5:22–23)? What would it mean in each of these three situations for the husband to function as head of his wife and for the wife to submit? Sometimes we are forced to think more clearly about biblical teaching when we have to apply it to specific circumstances.

Should the husband who wants to relocate do his best to wisely consider every relevant factor, including all that might be triggering his wife's emotional resistance, and then make a decision? Is that what headship means? And does submission require his wife to pack her bags without complaint if he decides to move?

How about the couple whose phone stopped ringing after ruining their evening? Should they hold a round table forum to prepare a strategy for handling similar occurrences? Perhaps they could take turns with anticipated responsibilities or assign them specifically to one or the other. And more open communication about churning resentments might help them to recognize areas of immaturity and selfishness and lead to a more generous spirit as they live together. Would that be mutual submission?

Should the man in the third situation seek professional help? Maybe the problems he faces with an irrationally angry wife cannot be remedied with the medicine of other-centered relating. But remember his observation that slamming the door seems, among the options he has tried, to most reliably improve her mood. Has he simply been too weak with her, perhaps placating her when stronger leadership was called for? Maybe his wife longs to feel secure in a strength she has never known, and therefore responds to even a poor counterfeit of what she wants. Should he therefore be more decisive than tender when she is upset, more directive than solicitous? Is that masculine leadership?

When we ask about headship and submission in the context of concrete marriage struggles, it is a little more difficult to discuss our positions with glib confidence. Thinking about actual situations may help us to focus the discussion and to more clearly recognize the central issues.

# THE HEART OF THE DEBATE

Before we can understand what headship and submission might mean in situations like these, we must move to the heart of the debate and first answer one basic question: Does a husband possess a God-given authority in marriage that his wife does not possess?

This is perhaps the central issue that divides us in our views on marriage. For centuries, Bible students have wrestled with the meaning of the word *head*. Does its use in Scripture carry the force of "authority over someone" or does it really mean something very different, such as "source" with no hint of authority?

Whichever view one takes on this question, most of us agree that one partner should not dominate the other or issue military-style orders. Whatever *headship* means, it does not mean "tyranny." Even though the Greek word Paul used for *submit* was sometimes used in a military setting, only the extreme traditionalists (and may their numbers decrease) think that wives should mindlessly obey their husbands the way a private responds to the commands of his sergeant.

Reasonable advocates of both positions insist that mutual servanthood is a central issue that must never be compromised by one spouse selfishly asserting *any* kind of power—financial, emotional, sexual, or intellectual—over another. John Piper, for example, representing a balanced traditional perspective, teaches that "mature masculinity expresses itself not in the demand to be served but in the strength to serve and to sacrifice for the good of the woman."[1]

A position statement by a nontraditional group expresses a similar thought: "In the Christian home, husband and wife are to defer to each other in seeking to fulfill each other's preferences, desires, and aspirations. Neither spouse is to seek to dominate the other, but each is to act as servant of the other, in humility considering the other as better than oneself."[2]

On this point, most Christians agree. Disagreements surface when we try to understand the proper course of action married partners should follow when they hold opposing views on the same issue, for example, on disciplining a rebellious teen or attending a different church.

Husbands and wives should, of course, communicate openly and honestly. And such honesty needs to be bounded by sensitive love, where each person works hard to understand both the other's point of view and whatever deeper concerns may lie beneath the disagreement. Sincere efforts to listen in an atmosphere of mutual submission may lead to a happy resolution satisfying to both parties.

But what happens when it doesn't?* Should a couple appeal to a third person and submit to binding arbitration in order to avoid one spouse

---

*Marriages in which the partners live intimately with one another rarely move through disagreement with calm efficiency. When two people determine to put together a real marriage, things will often be stormy. Efficiency is more often a sign of distance, not maturity. Communication between husband and wife rarely leads to a negotiated solution. Instead, it creates an opportunity for real love to show itself through sacrifice. I therefore find little profit in most instructions about communication techniques.

deciding for both in a strongly contested matter? Or is there an authority structure within marriage, a final court of appeal, within which one partner exercises decision-making power?

Traditionalists and egalitarians differ on many issues, but none have more immediate and definite implications for married couples than the way they answer this big question: Does the husband have an authority to lead that the wife does not have?

Traditionalists answer, "Yes, he does!" He may not always use it, and whenever he does he must remain deeply sensitive to his wife's interests, but he is the final authority in the home. In John Piper's words, mature masculinity "accepts the burden of the final say in disagreements between husband and wife but does not presume to use it in every instance."[3]

Egalitarians answer, "No, he does not." In their understanding, marriage is a relationship between sexually distinct but fully equal human beings. This equality should be recognized by dividing the responsibilities of leadership not on the basis of gender, but "on the basis of gifts, expertise, and availability."[4] Neither partner has authority over the other. "In cases of decisional deadlock, [husband and wife] should seek resolution through biblical methods of conflict resolution rather than by one spouse imposing a decision upon the other."[5]

## A THIRD ANSWER

These two answers seem to be the only options. But perhaps there is a third answer, one that may have important elements in common with both traditionalists and egalitarians but that brings a few additional perspectives into sharper focus. This third answer, that best fits my understanding of the biblical ideal, might be expressed as follows:

> Husbands and wives both have authority in marriage. Their authority is equal in responsibility; that is, it is not like a captain's authority over a sergeant or a sergeant's authority over a private. Husbands and wives have the authority to serve one another in wisdom and love. Married partners are authorized by God to give themselves to their mates. This is their authority.
>
> However, because the sexes are distinct in what they were fundamentally designed to give and in what brings them the greatest joy in relationship, the expression of their authority should reflect those distinctions. At the deepest level, a man serves a woman differently than a woman serves a man. Headship, the expression of a man's authority to serve, is characterized by rich involvement and by leadership that includes making decisions to resolve an impasse. Submission, the expression of a woman's authority to serve, is characterized by invitation and supportiveness.

This lengthy statement requires clarification. My direct answer to the central question—does a husband possess an authority that his wife does not?—is no and yes. *No*, it is not true that husbands possess authority and wives have none. Each has been granted equal authority under God to serve the other. Authority is fundamentally authority to serve, not to lead.

But *yes*, there is a difference. The authority of a husband to serve his wife is distinct from the authority of a wife to serve her husband. The distinction in authority is not imposed by fiat, it rather grows out of distinctive resources for service in men and women.

It is misleading to define *headship* as a husband's right to decide something for his wife and then to require her submissive cooperation with his decision. Defining headship centrally as decision-making authority puts the wife in a position of subordination to a despotic authority. It creates a kind of hierarchical arrangement that blocks the growth of intimacy. Order is achieved at the expense of passion.

But it does not therefore follow that neither husband nor wife has a unique responsibility for leadership. Because of their differences, husbands and wives express their authority to serve differently.

A husband's authority to *wisely serve* his wife with the *resources of his masculinity**  requires that he involve himself deeply in the affairs of his family and that he serve them as advocate. It requires that he provide them with love and direction in accordance with his understanding of God's character and their needs.

A wife exercises her authority to serve by prayerfully evaluating how her unique resources as a

---

*Notice again the two elements that go into any decision on how to serve one's mate: (1) a wise understanding of what the other was designed to enjoy and (2) an appreciation of one's own unique resources as a man or woman to provide this enjoyment.

woman can best encourage her husband as he moves into his home and work. And as she uses her abilities to advance God's purposes through her life, she will remain sensitive to her unique (and therefore priority) opportunity to minister deeply to her husband. She is not required to mechanically obey her husband but rather she is wonderfully equipped to serve her husband and free to do so wisely. A wife serves her husband by offering him nondemanding respect and being strongly and vulnerably *for* him in order to affirm his masculinity.

A wife and a husband's freedom and authority is the same: *to wisely use the personal resources of their sexual being on behalf of their spouse.*

Should a husband consistently demonstrate ungodly behavior, his wife's responsibility is to submit to God's purposes without angrily demanding that her husband change (1 Peter 3:1—6). Her actual response to her husband could range from full cooperation to a clear refusal to cooperate. She would refuse to cooperate, for example, if he were to ask her to engage in perverted sex or if he were to abuse her physically. She needs to judge what would best promote godliness in her husband.

This understanding of authority in marriage raises a number of discussable issues, two of special interest to me.

First, this understanding of authority places responsibility for behavior squarely on the shoulders of each spouse. Neither can say, "He/she made me do it." And wherever people are given the freedom to exercise their authority as they see fit, this freedom will be abused.

For example, the husband in Marriage #1 may reason that it's really best for his wife if they relocate. He may persuade himself that she has an unhealthy dependence on her parents that is interfering with her growth as a mature wife and mother. A selfish decision to advance his own career may therefore be disguised as a responsible exercise of his authority to serve.

The wife's determination to stay put may similarly prejudice her assessment of things. She may conclude that supporting her husband in his desire to move would in fact strengthen materialistic leanings that could one day consume him and thereby she might justify her refusing to move as a godly exercise of her authority to serve.

By introducing the idea of a mutual authority to serve that involves freely chosen but sexually distinct expressions of that authority, do we create the potential for more sophisticated forms of marriage abuse than male tyranny and blatant self-promotion? How can husbands and wives learn to exercise their mutual authority without disguising rank selfishness beneath the cloak of ministry? That is the first issue I want to consider.

Second, this understanding of authority presupposes that men and women really are different at very deep levels of their being, both in what they uniquely have to give and in what they especially long to receive. We have already discussed some of the important differences between the sexes and why I am persuaded they exist. What we need to do yet is think carefully about how serving one another in marriage can take those differences into account.

In the rest of this chapter we'll look at the first issue; in the last two chapters we'll discuss the second.

## STANDARDS TO FOLLOW
## OR A NEW DESIRE?

The notion of equal authority to serve with distinct expression leaves husbands and wives with a large measure of freedom to exercise their authority, and this goes against a common understanding of how to live the Christian life.

We sometimes think that God's job is simply to tell us what to do, and our job is first to figure out what he said and then to try very hard to do what we're told. Successful Christian living, in this way of thinking, comes down to two key elements: *God's holy standards*, reflecting his perfect character, and *our moral effort*, indicating our commitment to obedient discipleship.

Our first job then, if this view were correct, is to better understand the standards by which we must abide.

Often, we depend on Bible students to determine precisely what God has said about matters such as headship and submission. Because Bible students sometimes come to opposite conclusions despite similar training in the work of interpretation, people tend to loyally stick to one teacher to avoid confusion. As a result, thousands of sincere Christians eagerly sit week after week under preachers and teachers who devote most of their sermons to telling people what God wants them to do.

"Husbands, lead your families," exhorts one teacher. "Wives, come alive with your freedom to be who you are," shouts another.

And every Sunday at noon the clearly taught saints march resolutely out of church, determined by the grace of God to live as they should or to be all they can be. A week later they return, feeling disappointed in themselves and a bit ashamed (a few with less self-awareness are proud of their achievements). They sense an angry discomfort as they sit with other folks who, judging by the force with which they sing the hymns and the rapt attention they give to the preacher, appear more spiritually successful.

The root of the trouble is an approach to Christian living that essentially depends on knowing God's ideas about things and working very hard to honor them. When those two elements are treated as the core ingredients in becoming mature, our churches will eventually resemble first-century synagogues run by Pharisees who carefully and with self-conscious piety teach the law (can you imagine a Pharisee ever telling his congregation that he was currently struggling with personal sin?). They will be filled with either weary folks who know that their best efforts fall short but are willing to try harder again next week, or proud people who, like their teachers, so badly miss the point of God's law that they think they are keeping it and eagerly parade their maturity before others as a worthy example.

This approach to Christian living is deadly.

I wonder how many women struggle every day to submit to insensitive, sometimes cruel husbands, believing that submission is another law to keep, another burdensome principle to observe, another weight of duty God piles on already bent shoulders. I wonder, too, as they try their hardest to do whatever they think submission requires, how many panic over ugly feelings and thoughts that emerge from somewhere inside them. Perhaps they long for either their husbands' death or their own, or they secretly hope another woman might seduce their husband and thereby release them from marital bondage.

How many husbands are determined not to interfere with their wives' freedom, believing that their primary responsibility as men involves enabling rather than leading. And how many, as they applaud their wives' achievements, battle privately against sexual temptations, sometimes perverted, always strong, that promise to relieve an empty space within, or against feelings of inadequacy that feed a competitive spirit or encourage a safe retreat. I wonder how many of these men have overcome temptation by cutting the nerve endings to their masculine souls and live out their lives as spiritual eunuchs, with a displayed competence that draws no one to enjoy their strength.

Before we worry whether the Bible teaches a traditional understanding of marriage or an egalitarian one, we must rid ourselves of this heretical notion that Christian living consists of nothing more than trying hard to keep standards. Whichever set of marital standards we accept, as long as we regard them as rules to follow or principles to observe, we will know little of true freedom or joy. Our lives will be characterized more by rigid conformity or liberated selfishness than by humble passion.

The gospel introduces us to an entirely new perspective on what it means to live by standards. In fact, it makes the standards so much a part of us that the key to relating well is not in following a set of well-studied principles, but in cooperating with desires that arise from within our hearts when we are walking in close fellowship with Christ.

This is a dramatic shift. Without the gospel, the best we could manage was living according to imposed principles with as much consistency as our natures would allow. We lived "under the law." We had to interpret the meaning of words chiseled into stone or written on a page, apply the teaching to our circumstances ("What do I do when I'm comfortably nestled into a chair and the phone rings?"), and then square our shoulders and resolve to do the right thing. The important thing was to clearly define, then faithfully apply, biblical principles for living.

But the gospel has turned the whole thing around. Biblical principles still need to be understood and obeyed, but Christian living now depends on the change God has made inside of us. And this change, though often unfelt and unnoticed, is profound.

## A REMARKABLE CHANGE

Other people—pastors, friends, spouses, parents—can influence my behavior. They can exhort me to live in good ways. They can ask things of me or scold me or encourage me or attempt to persuade me on certain matters. They can provide me with various pleasures or tempt me with them. They can help me understand what is going on within me and clarify connections between past events and present reactions.

But what they cannot do is change my heart.

When a parent sets the standard for the cleanliness of a teenage daughter's room, two opposing forces are set in motion: the *parent's intention* as expressed in the declared standard and the *teenager's intention* to do what she wants. As long as these two forces are at odds, parent and daughter will never enjoy sitting together in the daughter's room.

Discipline, scolding, promises of wrath to come (with an occasional advance taste), generous expressions of material kindness—nothing that the parent can ever do will make a deep and enduring difference. At best, the room may be treated to a cosmetic clean-up—everything visible in good order. But a closer inspection beneath the bed and behind the dresser will make it clear that the girl's heart was not in the project.

No one changes the human heart. No one disturbs the center of my being where passionate energy continues to move in self-centered directions. No one except Christ.

When Christ goes to work, he gets right to the heart of the matter, literally. He tears out my old heart and puts in a new one (Ezek. 36:26). And then, rather than standing outside and telling me what to do with it, he moves inside and directs things from there. He still has laws for me to keep and principles to follow; but now the laws are not merely imposed from without, they arise from within. God's law is now written on our hearts (Jer. 31:33).

Because we embrace the lawgiver and are embraced by him in a relationship so intimate that we actually "participate in the divine nature"

(2 Peter 1:4),* we want more than ever to keep his laws, but now we see their deeper dimension. We come to realize that biblical principles reflect the heart of someone we love and trust, and we receive his directions, not as required duties (though, of course, they are), but rather as welcome opportunities to live as he intends, knowing that our good is always on his mind. Only with this understanding of things can we say with the psalmist: "I run in the path of your commands, for you have set my heart free; . . . how I long for your precepts; . . . how I love your law; . . . your statutes are . . . the joy of my heart; my heart is set on keeping your desires to the very end" (Psalm 119: 32, 40, 97, 111, 112).

The gospel frees us from the burden of always living by standards that feel imposed. When we come to the Bible, we can expect to find principles for living that promote a sense of freedom within our souls rather than ones that chain us to our duties. As we grasp that we live our lives as forgiven sinners, as unworthy servants, as purchased slaves, we will be less inclined to redefine biblical teaching to accommodate the ambitions of a much-loved self. Rather than changing the law to fit our hearts, Christ has changed our hearts to fit his law.

Either we live by external standards in the

---

*The more we understand God's passion for intimate relationship, the more we will warmly regard sexual intercourse as not only pleasurable but also richly expressive of the life-sharing and deeply satisfying union between Christ and his church. How God must hate adultery, rape, sexual abuse, premarital relations! How he must grieve when married couples experience pleasureless sex, idolized sex, pressured sex, manipulative sex, or mechanical sex!

strength of moral effort, with grace as a warmly regarded side issue, or we live by grace in the strength of a new heart, enjoying the law as a needed and welcome guide and no longer hating it as a crushing weight.

When we approach the topic of headship and submission from the first perspective, we become *law-keepers* who frantically sweat to do what we should and end up defeated with good reason or proud without reason; or we become *law-breakers* who in our self-exalting determination to rid ourselves of unnatural restraints learn to hate boundaries more than love God.

But, when we approach our marriage responsibilities in the freedom of our new relationship to God's standards, we will measure the accuracy of our biblical understanding by continued study of the text and we will determine the impact of the text, in part, by how deeply we are moved to serve our mates with the joyful passion of a consuming interest in their well-being.

Headship and submission are best understood as sexually distinctive expressions of an equal authority, the authority to serve. But this mutual authority to devote the unique resources of manhood and womanhood to the sexually distinct longings of our mates can be abused. Wherever there is freedom, there will be abuse.

The biblical safeguards against abuse do not consist of either removing freedom by tightening authority into well-defined roles as in a traditional relationship or removing authority and emphasizing self-expression as in an egalitarian relationship.

It is better to deal with the potential abuse of freedom by promoting a deeper appreciation of the gospel. Forgiven sinners with new hearts, who are growing in the wonder of what the gospel has done and will yet do, do a better job of handling their freedom than folks with either controlled hearts or unrestrained hearts.

With confidence in the gospel and with a determination to root all our teaching about marriage in the freedom of the gospel, we must be prepared to arrive at an understanding of headship and submission that encourages husbands and wives to sense their responsible liberty to move in whatever directions they deeply desire to move as men and women who are forgiven by God, who rejoice in the uniqueness of their sexuality, who value the uniqueness of their spouses' sexuality, and who passionately long to affirm their mate as a man or woman.

It is impossible to develop a set of principles that can be adequately translated into a clear response to every potential situation in a marriage. It is *not* impossible to develop an appreciation of the gospel that, coupled with an understanding of God's principles for living, moves us to respond to every situation with maturing wisdom and love.

# *Eleven*

## Relating as Men and Women

*There is no such thing in the world as liberty, except under the law of liberty; that is, the essential laws of our own being, not our feelings which come and go.*

GEORGE MACDONALD

*What, then, are we to do? Too many marriages are* simply not working. And even the good ones, where couples feel deeply the touch of love, fall woefully short of enjoying all that marriage was meant to provide. Tensions surface unexpectedly, tempers flare into harsh words whose sting lasts for years, kisses of greeting feel routine, and the unmistakable chill of distance is more often felt than the warmth of a bedtime hug.

Think back to the three brief scenarios described in the previous chapter. In Marriage #1, an opportunity to relocate divided the husband and wife into warring factions, with each side feeling misunderstood, unsupported, and bitter. The partners in Marriage #2 heard the phone ring during an uneventful evening of watching TV and, even though exhausted, they both within seconds found the energy to hate. In Marriage #3, a young wife flew into uncontrollable rage at the slightest provocation. Her bewildered husband has no idea how best to respond. She feels trapped by irrational emotions; he feels helpless and resentful.

If these couples, and countless others like them who privately endure the confusing pain of imperfect and sometimes awful marriages, are ever going to know the gladness of love and the joy of intimacy, something more basic than trying to handle the immediate problem needs to be done.

Before we try to understand what course of action each spouse should follow in these situations, I would first like to ask a seemingly irrelevant question: *What overwhelms you more fully than anything else?*

I sometimes wonder if I have ever been overwhelmed more by my selfishness than by my hurt over rejection or failure. Do I know what it is to be reduced to face-down humility by the staggering fact that God has not given up on me, that the one who knows me as no one else does is still smiling? Or am I really more bothered, and frankly irritated, with the way he sometimes withholds blessings and greets with silence my pleas of anguish during rough times in my life? Am I grateful and content only when he comes through as I want, and impatiently puzzled the rest of the time? Let me illustrate.

Recently, after a few months of an unusually hectic speaking and travel schedule, I felt burned out. My energy disappeared, the spark was gone.

Discouragement slipped into resentment of folks who continued to want something from me. Requests from friends for personal advice, invitations to speak at yet another conference, everyday responsibilities like paying bills pressed in on me with suffocating force. Simple requests from my wife, like asking that I return a suitcase to its spot in the closet, seemed an intolerable burden.

During periods like these, my mind will not shut down. It races with feverish and thoroughly non-productive intensity toward every problem in my life—real, anticipated, or imagined. Sleep becomes difficult. Sometimes, in the middle of the night, I'll crawl out of bed and slump on the living room couch, with an open Bible, and read aimlessly, begging God to restore calmness to my soul and sleep to my body.

Sometimes it works, and I feel better after an hour of tearful petition. More often, it doesn't, and I return to bed only because it's warmer under covers than on the couch.

Why doesn't God come through? Where is the peace he promises? At those moments it seems to me that the overwhelming pressure I feel should provoke God to do something. And then it becomes clear that I tend to be more overwhelmed with my struggles (and therefore demand relief) than with my opportunities to touch at least a few people well, opportunities that are blocked only by my self-centeredness.

If we are to understand the best thing to do during moments of conflict, we must first be overwhelmed with both the horror of our self-centeredness and the wonder of God's grace. Only then will there be any genuine stirring of other-centeredness that can be wisely channeled.

When we are more gripped by the sheer wrongness and pervasiveness of our self-centeredness and by the incomparable beauty of God's grace than by the pain caused by another's unkindness, then the Spirit of God does something wonderful. We begin to feel moved, in the deepest regions of our being, to care about someone else more than ourselves and to be more passionately committed to knowing God than to finding immediate relief from our pain (Ezek. 36:24–27).

One evidence that we are being "moved to follow his decrees" (Ezek. 36:27) is our noticing things about our partner that we formerly failed to see. We begin to recognize what our spouse would love to receive from us, and we are excited when we realize that we can give what he or she longs to receive.

Husbands in whom the Spirit is working look tenderly at their wives, knowing how badly women want to feel special and enjoyed. Cherishing their wives becomes more important than getting ahead in business. And wives sense how inadequate their husbands sometimes feel, and how much their support and respect would mean to them. They begin to see through the social confidence and the angry moodiness to the desperate desire to feel strong and to matter. And, as the Spirit continues to move, men and women spend more time thinking about how they affect each other than about their own personal fulfillment.

If this process is developing in our hearts (and it will develop when the right things overwhelm us), we can profitably ask how to best handle a conflict over relocating, or tension generated by an unanswered phone, or hypersensitivity in one partner that neither knows how to relieve. To understand what to do in specific situations like these, husbands and wives need to look closely at each other to find out what each wants that the other can provide.

Because I'm far more concerned with the condition of our hearts than with what we actually do, I hesitate to offer specific illustrations of what headship and submission might require of marriage partners in specific situations. Developing a right heart, which out of brokenness releases other-centered energy, is a far more important and difficult process than coming up with a list of practical suggestions and trying to implement them.

Addressing the reality of selfishness in both spouses' hearts is my first concern in building a marriage. Consider the implications of this idea for the three marriages already mentioned.

## MARRIAGE #1

Recall the situation in the first example. The husband (let's call him Pete) wants to relocate for the sake of his career. His wife Beth wants to remain close to her parents for the sake of the children. What would other-centeredness look like in this situation?

The first move of a manly husband would *not* be to make a decision and force it on his wife. Recognizing his tendency toward self-centeredness and wanting to handle the situation with other-centered energy, Pete would first commit himself to being sensitive to Beth's feelings in all that he does. He would first try to explore and understand Beth's fears. The concern he expresses for her welfare would override his desires for vocational advance.

If he sensed an angry or demanding spirit within himself that seemed deeper than his determination to love his wife well, he would face the fact that he is in no spiritual state to make a nonreversible decision. His first order of business would be to deal with his self-centeredness through soul-searching (perhaps including counseling), fervent prayer, reflective time in the Bible, and eventually repentance. Engaging in these activities would be a legitimate exercise of headship.

How would Beth react? In Pete's movement toward her, Beth would feel either a commitment to her well-being or she would sense how disturbed Pete felt over his lack of proper commitment. She wouldn't feel manipulated or pressured to merely accede to a demand. Rather, deep parts within her that reflexively tighten whenever personal danger is sensed would relax, and she would find pleasure in his concern to treat her well. She would feel free both to express herself to an advocate and to invite further movement toward her, knowing she was enjoyed and respected. Beth would communicate her respect for him and her willingness to warmly cooperate with any decision he chooses to make, including a move.

This rare and ideal but possible exercise of equal yet different authority would create a climate of trust in which Pete and Beth would place God's eternal purposes and their relationship above career advancement or proximity to grandparents. The interplay of Pete's sensitive involvement with an enjoyed wife and Beth's warm reception of a valued husband might resolve the problem.

But if it doesn't, and often it won't, Pete should not then reach for a badge of authority to justify an exercise of headship. He should rather continue to exercise his masculine authority to serve his wife by providing clear leadership. He would make a decision. And Beth, rather than grumpily realizing she is now supposed to submit, would continue to exercise her feminine authority to serve her husband by warmly cooperating with his decision.

The exercise of authority does not begin at the point of unresolvable conflict; it simply continues. Serving each other as man and woman is the key, not acting out the roles of leader and follower.

What happens, however, when one of them handles the same situation with self-centered immaturity? Suppose Beth refuses to talk, accuses her husband of not caring about the kids, and angrily cries whenever he mentions moving. Suppose, too, that Pete reacts with other-centered maturity. He patiently and nondefensively listens to her tirades and finds the strength not to retaliate, aggressively push his own way, or weakly retreat. What then?

There is no principle that can be translated into normative and clear advice such as: "Headship means you must go ahead and decide. Call the moving van and start packing. If she resists, don't back down!" or "Keep on praying until God moves your wife to an attitude that will enable you to be of one mind. God never leads husbands and wives separately. Wait for him to work."*

---

*Refusing to offer a definite direction to the husband evidences neither a moral cowardice nor an unwillingness to enforce biblical injunctions. It rather reflects the awareness that dependence on the Holy Spirit working in a redeemed heart can easily be replaced by biblical-sounding human wisdom that prefers controlling behavior to releasing people to their God-given freedom.

The husband's job is to remain sensitive to self-centered patterns in his relating, to reflect long and hard (perhaps with help) on his wife, and to pray earnestly for wisdom. And then, in light of all that he comes to understand about himself, his wife, and God's will, he must use his authority as servant-head to make a decision according to what he determines will further God's purposes in his family.

He may choose to sign a contract to start his job in a new location in six months. He may choose to remain where he is and devote the next thirty years to more richly loving Beth in the same house. Either option, and many others, could be right. The decision on how to exercise his authority to serve his wife is his to make. And he must make it. If Pete is aware of a deep and sincere desire to satisfy Beth's longing to be enjoyed by a strong advocate, then he has reason to trust his heart as he asks God to control his decision.

Suppose now that it is Pete who proves demanding and churlish. What does submission require Beth to do? The answer cannot be confined to one pre-set reaction lest submission be wrongly reduced to a simple principle such as, "Do whatever you're told except when it would involve clear sin." Because a wife must devote her resources to blessing her husband, then she, like the husband married to a stubborn wife, has the responsibility to make a wise decision.

Now it is at this point that the primary emphasis of this book again comes into focus. Unless Beth is living in the enjoyment of a relationship with Christ that makes her willing to dedicate all that she is and has to God's purposes for her husband, encouraging her to do whatever she thinks best will open the door to every form of refined selfishness. This is why the first concern in building a marriage is not defining submission or headship, but addressing the reality of selfishness in both spouses' hearts until the celebration of their forgiveness creates a hunger to follow God with all their heart, soul, mind, and strength and to spend their lives in service to others, especially their mates.

Beth is accountable to God for her real motivation as she chooses her course of action. At the judgment day, her decision will be measured by the degree to which it came out of a sincere desire to exercise her authority to serve her husband by devoting her womanly resources to encouraging godly manhood in him (1 Cor. 4:5). It is up to her to do all that she can as a woman to have a godly influence on her man.

An important question arises as Beth decides what specific form her other-centered service will assume: Is she free to refuse to cooperate with her husband's direction? In this situation, could it be in God's will for Beth to be unwilling to move?

Most of us agree that submission never requires a wife to support her husband by following him into sin. But why? Does she refuse to cooperate with a husband's sinful wishes only because she's obeying a higher authority? In this view, a wife whose husband directs her to assist him in embezzling funds would say no because God's Word makes it clear that stealing is wrong. And that, of course, is adequate reason for her to say no.

But there's another rationale for a wife's not cooperating with her husband's sin. She would not cooperate because doing so would be a poor exercise of her authority to bless her husband and thereby violate God's design for her life. To be a partner in embezzling funds is wrong on two counts: it involves her in clearly immoral activity, and it encourages her husband in ungodly leadership.

The second view provides a framework for thinking through what a wife should do when her husband's leadership does not involve either him or her in obvious sin, but still appears unwise to her because it reflects more subtle sinfulness.

In my judgment, a wise exercise of a wife's authority would generally be to encourage her husband by cooperating with his questionable plans with a quiet and gracious spirit (1 Peter 3:1–6). However, I can envision a situation where loving wisdom would lead her to act in a fashion that would confront him with the negative consequences of his decision.

Beth may decide to pack her bags with cheerful grace. Or, she may clearly lay out her objections to the move and indicate that if he still wants to move after considering her perspective for two weeks, she will move. If, after extensive prayer and frank feedback from godly people about her attitude, she determines that agreeing to a move is strengthening something clearly bad in her husband, she may be persuaded that not relocating would better serve God's purpose in her husband's life. It is my view, however, that the hardness involved in a husband's poor decision would best be softened *not* by the refusal of a wife to cooperate but rather by her willingness to support him even when their judgment differs.

Any one of these directions could represent

godly submission. Her authority to serve her partner is hers to exercise before God. She is to serve
her husband as she obeys God's command to do
so. She must decide not whether she should submit to her husband, but rather what a submissive
yielding of herself to God's purposes would mean
in this situation.

## MARRIAGE #2

Remember the wife (let's refer to her as Miriam)
who angrily wondered if she was supposed to
answer the phone "just because he tells me to."
What would submission to a petulant husband
who regarded his fatigue as sufficient reason to
expect his wife to wait on him look like?

This illustration makes it clear why neither traditional views about roles and rules, nor modern
views that emphasize equality address the core
problem that is robbing Miriam of joy. Persuading
Miriam to answer the phone the next time it rings
because this is what a wife should do fails to deal
with her self-centered energy. It runs the risk of
imposing a legal requirement on an unchanged
person. Paul's discussion of the law's inability to
produce holy living (Romans 7) should make us
question this advice.

Encouraging Miriam to establish personal
boundaries within which she can regard herself as
equal in value to her husband similarly misses the
point. When we work at developing a good self-
image as a basis for becoming more loving people,
somehow most of us end up spending almost all
our energy on learning to like ourselves better.

Sacrificial kindness to others becomes a noble but always future ambition.

For Miriam, submission would first require a disturbing look at her own attitude and agenda. If Miriam's husband is badly insensitive (and the illustration makes it clear that he is), then Miriam might be tempted to use his insensitivity as an excuse for her own self-centeredness. She would need to think about this until she was gripped more by her own sin than by his and until she was grateful more for God's grace than for any hope of her husband changing.

With those other-centered dynamics in place, Miriam should be encouraged to notice what her husband desires. Asking him what she could do that he would deeply appreciate might begin the process of encouraging him. As she invites him to enjoy what she can give, it would be entirely appropriate for her to let him know that she some-times feels used and to suggest ways for him to love her better.

If she were learning to give to him and to share openly with him, then perhaps the next time the phone required attention from one of two tired people, she would be willing to answer it, not because he told her to, but because she wanted to.


## MARRIAGE #3

In our third situation, a husband (call him Kent) is frustrated with his wife's frequent episodes of irra-tional anger. As with every situation involving con-flict, we must spend ninety percent of the work on shifting from self-centeredness that feels justified to other-centeredness that flows naturally from a repentant heart.

If we assume that Kent is meaningfully other-centered and sincerely desirous of helping his wife, then it might be proper for him to insist forcefully that they go together for counseling. But before he moves in this direction, I would encourage him to study both his reaction to her and her reaction to him in the hopes of discerning hidden hurt within Michelle to which he could more gently respond.

Perhaps she has never felt safe enough with him to discuss her memories of sexual abuse. Or perhaps her grandmother spent her life in a mental hospital, and Michelle is terrified that this same fate awaits her. With the modern emphasis on counseling, it is easy to turn to a counselor too quickly and to overlook the power of a husband's gentle but penetrating involvement with the wounds of his wife. Good husbanding may have more effect than good counseling.

Kent might also exercise headship by clearly defining what he will and will not do for Michelle. She may be using her irrational behavior to control Kent in ways that nothing else will achieve.

The range of action that Kent might appropriately take is wide. Whatever he does, however, must reflect his desire to provide the strength of a relentlessly caring advocate, a strength that will survive whatever heartache Michelle brings into his life. If she were to become suicidal or homicidal or abusive of either Kent or their kids, then responsible advocacy could include whatever legal or medical measures prove necessary to prevent a tragedy.

❊  ❊  ❊

I hope these illustrations have given you some idea about how husbands can exercise headship and wives can exercise submission in the midst of marital conflict. Because headship and submission are more an expression of who we are than a statement of what we should do, it is difficult to define the terms clearly and easy to misunderstand them badly. But let me risk an attempt at defining them in the next and last chapter.

# *Twelve*

## Enjoying the Difference

*I used to think that being nice to people and feeling nice was loving people. Now I know it isn't. Love is the most immense unselfishness and it is so big I've never touched it.*

FLORENCE ALLSHORN

*Perhaps the most common misunderstanding of marriage* responsibilities involves an authoritarian view of male leadership in the home. Conservative Christians tend to think of headship as a kind of "authority-in-reserve," a badge that sits in the husband's desk drawer until the power it symbolizes is needed. When trouble begins and direction is required, the head of the home reaches into the drawer for his badge, pins it on his chest, and settles things with a manly display of decisive leadership.

But, as we saw with Pete and Kent, the masculine version of serving a woman, of a man giving a woman what she longs to receive from him, allows no room for the notion of authority as despotic power over another that somehow belongs to the office of husband. God does not grant authority to the "position" of husband and then permit whomever occupies that position to use this authority whenever he sees fit without a priority concern to serve the well-being of his wife. The authority of a husband is not an "authority-in-reserve." It is not a badge that, when pinned to his chest, makes him a sheriff.

## TOWARD UNDERSTANDING HEADSHIP

Headship is a distinctive form of the authority to serve that belongs to the husband, not simply because he is the husband, but because he is a man, because he is masculine. A husband exercises headship over a wife when he expresses his manhood toward her, when he gently but strongly leads her with a strength that is not afraid to become deeply involved and with a maintained sense of direction that expresses strongly held convictions. Headship is not a badge to quickly grab when a decision must be made. It is a way of relating that reflects a husband's masculinity as he engages with his wife's femininity.

Let me try to explain what I mean. A man longs to feel complete. Whether single or married, he wants to know that he can move toward a woman and touch her deeply. Clearly, what I'm talking about goes beyond financial provision and sexual pleasures. The former could be supplied by the death of a wealthy aunt, and the latter requires only the physical capacity of a male body; neither defines the exercise of manhood. In order to exercise his manhood (which in marriage is the same thing as headship), a man must understand both what a woman was uniquely designed to enjoy and that he has what it takes to provide her with that enjoyment. Think with me first about what a woman was uniquely designed to enjoy.

Imagine the pleasure that rushed through Eve's entire being when Adam first approached her. After looking at animals for so long, Adam must have been ecstatic when he saw a woman, naked, beautiful, inviting. Adam's delight was more than sexual. Certainly sexual arousal must have been wonderfully present, but Adam's enjoyment of Eve extended to every level of relationship. Marriage was never intended to be a relationship between two persons who happen to have complementary physical shapes appropriate only for sexual activity. It is rather a relationship between a man and woman whose *personal shapes* are as enjoyably different as their physical shapes.

Had Adam felt aroused only by the prospect of physical pleasure, Eve, like so many wives today, would have eventually felt used and unwanted as a person, rightly offended by a lust for her body that took little interest in her soul. But Adam's enjoyment of Eve was undoubtedly an enjoyment of all that she had to offer.

A woman wants to know that the deepest parts of her being are richly enjoyed by a man who will therefore treat her with tenderness and look at her with delight, someone who will enjoy her because she is enjoyable, not because of a manipulative desire that hopes to get from her what will bring pleasure to him.

But women have learned to be skeptical. Every little girl has discovered that not everything wonderful about her will be reliably enjoyed. Some of who she is will at times be ignored, despised, demeaned, or selfishly used. In a fallen world, she learns that offering all that she is to another runs the terrible risk of rejection and abuse. And because she too is fallen and therefore committed to her own well-being with no thought of dependence on God, she figures out how to minimize the risks by hiding the tenderest parts of her soul and avoiding an honest look at her ugly parts.

In order to survive in a world where people carelessly hurt her and use her for their own purposes, she learns to cover her delicate nature with a hard crust, a toughness always on the alert for dangers. When she is by herself long enough to reflect on what she really wants, she becomes at least vaguely aware (sometimes acutely to the point of despair) of how nice it would be if someone were tough *for* her. Deep within her being, she longs for an advocate, not a tyrant who would control her life with his strength, but an advocate whose strength on her behalf would free her to go "off duty" and to express more of who she really is. She longs for an advocate who would enjoy her and give her the hope that she could invite people into meaningful relationship with the confidence that there really was something about her that could be enjoyed.

A man, if he is to be richly sensitive to his wife, must know how much she wants to be enjoyed by an advocate whose tender strength frees her to give all that she is to others. But he must understand a second thing as well: that he can provide her with what she desires. This realization does not come easily.

When a man senses how badly his wife desires

an advocate and longs to be enjoyed, he often feels both angry and threatened: angry that she is needy when he feels needy himself and threatened because he is not at all persuaded that he has what she needs. He worries that perhaps his enjoyment of her would stir her very little, and he wonders if he could ever be strong in a way that would encourage her to relax in his strength rather than correct his mistakes. Perhaps he is simply not wise or strong or loving enough to set directions that any woman in her right mind would trust.

In order for a man to overcome his doubts, he must centrally do two things: (1) he must *focus on God* and all that it means to be forgiven, accepted, and called until he is persuaded that there is real strength in acknowledged weakness and until he is stirred in his redeemed heart to use that strength in other-centered relating. Clearly that will entail serious attention to Scripture and a dependent retreat to prayer. (2) He must *focus on his wife.* There is no better way to experience one's masculinity than for a redeemed heart that deeply cares to clearly see how badly a woman's heart longs for what only masculinity can provide. Strength that is pulled from a husband by the realization of his wife's longings is far more authentically masculine than strength that a man develops to prove he is a man.

Whatever insights a man may learn about himself by exploring his background and taking an inside look at his motives (a practice I heartily commend) must be thought about in the context of an even more determined look at God and his wife.

The more a man tends to accept his responsibilities as head of his home and to carry them out in godly fashion, the more he realizes that God has placed within him *exactly* what his wife longs to enjoy and what can encourage her to become all she was meant to be. It is important for a husband to know that his wife's highest calling from God is to invite others into relationship and that she is designed to enjoy meaning in life through attachments to others. When a man understands a woman, he is more likely to exercise his authority to serve, not by making occasional decisions or exhibiting his strength, but by being the advocate she desires and by moving tenderly toward her with a smile in his eyes that tells her she is enjoyed.

This understanding of headship corresponds nicely to Christ's headship. Christ is strongly (and sovereignly) involved with us in a fashion that conveys how wonderfully loved and graciously enjoyed we are as his bride in spite of the ugliness within that we're terrified to face. As we learn to relax in his advocacy and yield to his strength, we bear his fruit and reflect his beauty.

As Christ enters us with the strength of one who leads us through life, in some mysterious way he experiences a relational completeness not dissimilar to the completion a man feels as he strongly loves his wife. Listen to Paul: "And God placed all things under his feet and appointed him to be head over everything for the church, which is his body, the fullness of him who fills everything in every way" (Eph. 1:22–23).* Our Lord emptied himself of the trappings of deity in order to fill us with

---

*Wisdom, symbolizing our Lord, represented itself similarly: "I was rejoicing in his whole world and delighting in mankind" (Prov. 8:31).

himself, a union that somehow completes him as it restores us to cherished relationship.

A man is completed by filling something or someone that would be empty if he had not come. A woman is affirmed when someone whom she invites and who enjoys her enters her life. Headship then is a man's strong involvement with a woman—an involvement rooted in an awareness of the good effect he can have and in a deep enjoyment of all that his wife is and will yet become.

## TOWARD UNDERSTANDING SUBMISSION

Now, what is submission? Let me offer a simple description and then discuss it. Submission consists of a woman's warmly receiving and meaningfully supporting a man's involvement in life in a way that encourages his godliness.

The word that we translate *submit* covers "a complete range of meanings from submitting to an authority to a fully conscious putting oneself at the disposal of another."[1] Law-keepers like to highlight the idea of obedience and to downplay the more relational notion of someone thinking hard about how best to devote his resources to another's welfare. When the focus on two sexually distinct people working together to build a relationship is lost, submission is reduced to the requirement to do whatever you're told to do by someone in authority.

It is critical to keep our thinking closely tied up with a woman's chosen relationship with God and with her husband; otherwise we will regard submission as essentially a principle to follow or a role to enact rather than what it most fundamentally is, namely, an opportunity to touch a husband's masculinity with a wife's femininity. When we narrow submission into a principle of "following the leader" and lose sight of the dimension of freely giving available resources for perceived need, we must then hedge the principle with qualifications about when a wife is not required to follow.

Piper, for example, wisely argues that it is best *not to define submission in terms of specific behaviors,* but as "a *disposition* to yield to the husband's authority and an *inclination* to follow his leadership. She must never follow her husband's leadership into sin. She will not steal with him or get drunk with him or savor pornography with him or develop deceptive schemes with him." Submission, he indicates, "is a readiness to support his leadership wherever it does not lead to sin."[2]

Most agree that committing sin because your husband wants you to is never right. The principle is correct but it leaves a tricky question unresolved, one that we looked at briefly in the last chapter. Is a wife then required to cooperate with her husband's leadership in all cases where *obvious* sin is not involved? What happens when a wife's cosignature is required to secure a loan to purchase her husband's long-coveted sports car while a child's extensive dental work is being postponed due to lack of funds? How about a wife (like Beth) who is genuinely afraid that relocating for a better job reflects her husband's growing materialistic obsession, which is consuming more time at work and less time with a teenage son who is starting to hang out with the wrong crowd?

A wrong solution to the dilemma is to dismiss any notion of male authority as chauvinistic and biblically insupportable. This having been done, every decision can then be handled much as two business partners, each with fifty percent ownership of the stock, would determine marketing plans for their new product. The married partners, of course, are to operate within the framework of Christian love and that makes it clearly different from a merely business-type negotiation, but the *authority structure*, or lack of it, is the same in both situations.

In my understanding, this solution requires that we deny too much about sexual differences, creational order, trinitarian relational patterns, and biblical instructions about marriage. It also fails to adequately reckon with the core problem of self-centeredness, and therefore provides it with opportunity for expression.

A better solution (but not one without difficulties) is to define submission in more explicitly relational terms that accept masculine leadership as an essential and good element in biblical headship and grant to the woman an authority from God to intelligently, creatively, and sincerely serve her husband with the unique resources of her femininity, much as Beth tried to do in Marriage #1.

When we see that a wife's special resources as a woman consist primarily in an attitude of nourishing, unpanicked supportiveness and warm, non-biting acceptance, and that a husband's needs as a man have to do with worry over his adequacy to deeply matter in life, then the rhythm of the dance of relationship begins to be heard. Questions about cosigning a loan for a new sports car are no longer seen as problems to be resolved by applying principles or as issues to be resolved through intelligent negotiation. Rather, situations like these place a far greater demand for godliness on the wife and call for a deep trust in the Lord. She must now determine that her heart is right and pray for wisdom and a loving, other-centered spirit. Submitting to her husband requires more than conformity to a role or a willingness to speak up; it requires moving with a rhythm that only the humble and broken and rejoicing heart can hear.

Look at a few passages that point in this direction. "The wise woman builds her house, but with her own hands the foolish one tears hers down" (Prov. 14:1). "Better to live in a corner of the roof than share a house with a quarrelsome wife . . . Better to live in a desert than with a quarrelsome and ill-tempered wife" (Prov. 21:9, 19).

Foolish wives, presumably those wives who are nonsubmissive, rip apart their families with a nasty spirit. In his teaching on submission, Peter tells us what wisdom looks like in a woman. A wise woman, specifically one who is submissive, attracts her husband with the beauty of a gentle and quiet spirit, rather than drives him to the desert (1 Peter 3:1—4).

A quarrelsome and ill-tempered woman sees it as her job to keep things in order and feels distraught and deeply annoyed when she is unsuccessful. A gentle, quiet spirit is the fruit of resolving to follow God with unwavering settledness and therefore demanding nothing other than the opportunity to honor this purpose in all her relationships, realizing that only her own self-centeredness, never her husband, can rob her of that desired opportunity. She does not make it her goal to change her husband (although she fervently prays for needed change); her goal is rather to use all her resources in a fashion that has the power to draw her husband into stronger commitment to God and into more godly involvement with her.

Her authority to serve her husband must be exercised with a growing sensitivity to both her husband's needs and longings as a man and her unique resources as a woman. Consider first her husband's needs.

Every man, somewhere deep within his soul, struggles to feel adequate. It is true that some men, including forceful Christian leaders whose strength is more intimidating and distancing than attractive, would report no such struggle. Typically, they have covered over their worry with such a thick blanket of success (business, ministry, financial, athletic, and social) that the only evidence of internal inadequacy is a strength that seems more displayed than deep. Exhibited strength always has in mind one's own welfare and, as a result, is experienced by others as less than caring.

Most men, however, in moments of painful honesty, would admit to some uncertainty about their own effectiveness in achieving something of real value. The uncertainty is most acutely felt when a man sincerely wonders about his ability to meaningfully touch other people, especially his wife, and to win her respect and appreciation.

Ever since Adam first had to work up a sweat to make the ground yield more food than weeds, men have wondered if they have what it takes to get the job done. The question mark is inherited, passed on from father to son through an arrogant nature that is determined to find adequate resources within oneself.

When young boys move into their worlds and fail, a lesson is learned.

A man once told me of the time he helped his father build a workshop in their garage. He and his dad had cleaned the junk out of the garage and swept it clean. They had planned where they would put the work bench and where they would display the tools.

The next job to be completed was to hang the pegboard for the tools. When his dad realized he did not have enough pegs to hang all his tools, he decided to purchase them before hanging the board. While he was gone, his son, then a twelve-year-old boy, decided to surprise his dad by hanging the board by himself.

He had managed to secure the pegboard tightly to the wall in exactly the marked-out space, driving sturdy nails into the studs without bending even one. Just as he had stepped back to proudly survey the newly mounted board, his dad returned from the store. His dad's eye was immediately drawn to the spot where the electrical outlet was covered by the board. The boy had forgotten to cut out space to provide access for plugging in the tools.

"How could you forget about the outlets?" his dad yelled. "Now we'll have to yank all those nails out and probably tear up both the wall and the pegboard."

The boy learned his lesson, and as man remembered it: it is dangerous to move with initiative into one's world. In a fallen world, every decision, big or little, involves the uncertainty of possible failure.

When an other-centered woman discerns the deep questions that plague her husband as he carries on with life, no matter how confident or carefree he may seem, she will sense a desire within herself to respond to that question. If his treatment of her is unkind, she will, of course, struggle with a variety of other emotions as well, but as she understands her "authority to serve" as the defining purpose in her life, her new heart will respond, in at least some measure, to the unique opportunity for service her husband presents.

Not only must she clearly perceive the lingering questions in her husband's soul, but also she must become thankfully aware of her power to provide answers. What are her resources for touching her husband? A woman has been equipped to welcome others into relationship with her and to offer that welcome with a spirit secure enough to be nondemanding and confident enough to be thoroughly inviting.

Women typically withhold that part of themselves that has been abused or rejected or dismissed. And this part is what is central to their femininity, a warmly inviting spirit. Peter counsels women to give their husbands what a man finds most deeply attractive in a woman, a gentle and quiet spirit. Nothing more clearly responds to a man's questions about his own inadequacy than a woman who accepts him with unthreatened acceptance and inviting support, even when his judgment is poor.

A submissive wife will exercise her authority to

serve her husband with a spirit that encourages him in his manhood and with the joy that comes from giving oneself for the sake of another. A wife's submission is therefore a feminine expression of mutual submission that is one-way and nonreversible, just as a man's headship is a one-way and nonreversible masculine form of mutual submission.

## MORE THAN RULES

We must get over the idea that Christian living, in marriage or in any sphere of life, reduces to obeying a set of rules. There are, of course, standards to be kept, and keeping them requires effort, but our relationship with the standard-giver makes the burden of his authority both light and welcome (Matt. 11:28–30). God's standards are unyielding and tough, but their firmness feels harsh only when we fail to appreciate the privilege of relationship with him (and what it cost him to provide it) and regard our lives as ours to do with as we please.

Biblical principles for marriage should not be defined as a group of rules by which we are required to order our lives. Although there are standards and we are commanded to obey them, an emphasis on all that Christians must do can easily obscure the *point* of obedience, which is to build enjoyable relationships with God and with each other that demonstrate the reality of Jesus Christ to a world of hardened, unhappy people.

Talking about roles in marriage can similarly lead us in wrong directions in at least two ways.

First, working hard to define and live within our roles as husbands and wives encourages the legalistic streak in all of us; we sense more pressure to fit within boundaries than excitement because of the freedom to love our spouse.

Second, reducing marital responsibilities to roles may convey the impression that God has arbitrarily assigned people to jobs that need to be done rather than especially equipped them for tasks that provide opportunities for joyful living. Just as God calls people to work he has already enabled them to do, so he has designed men and women to relate in unique ways, and with his good plan in mind, he releases them to gladly accept their divinely appointed assignments. Talking about roles tends to obscure the idea of the "good and natural fit" that occurs when men and women live according to design.

Attempts to build a marriage by following rules or conforming to roles never quite produces a fluid, dynamic, natural union of two people becoming one. Something deeper is present in a good marriage.

## METAPHOR FOR A MARRIAGE

A really good marriage has the feel of a man and woman blending together into natural movement where individuality is obviously present but really isn't the point, something perhaps like dance partners of many years who anticipate each other's steps with practiced ease. (For those old enough to remember, picture Fred Astaire and Ginger Rogers gliding effortlessly across the floor in perfect harmony of movement.)

The rhythm of the music and the dancers' movements are two separate ingredients, and although it's clear that one directs the other, you don't sense that the dancers are working hard to keep in step with the music. The rhythm is *in* them; they move with it naturally, effortlessly, with every movement fitting the music because the music is part of them.

Beginning dancers have to think about moving as they should. Old-timers neither violate the rules nor work hard to follow them, but rather blend together their distinct contributions as each one responds to his or her own "feel" of the same music.

Years ago, as an older teen who had no idea how to dance, I found myself in a social dilemma. My girlfriend, now my wife, told me with excitement about a big event soon to be held on her college campus, an event that I knew would include dancing. My options were few: come down with a convenient sickness, and spoil her evening; go with her but insist she dance with other young men, and spoil my evening; or go with her and dance, and spoil both our evenings (and her feet).

I chose a fourth option: learn to dance before the event. I responded to a well-known studio's newspaper ad for three private introductory lessons. The day of the first lesson I remember climbing two flights of stairs to the dance studio on the third floor of an old brick building. When I reached the door, I paused to catch my breath and renew my determination to go through with the dancing lessons; then I responded to the invitation on the door to "Please Come In."

I was immediately greeted by a strikingly beautiful blonde woman, perhaps twenty-five years old, who introduced herself to me as "Tish." After a few pleasantries, I handed her a ten-dollar bill, and she took my hand and led me to the dance floor.

During this first lesson, held in a large room furnished with a record player and peopled only by me and my teacher, Tish instructed me to extend one of my arms to meet one of hers and to position my other arm around her waist. With these points of contact, she assured me, I could convey with gentle pressure both the direction I intended to move and the speed with which I was about to move in that direction. She then would follow my lead.

When I protested that I hadn't the slightest notion of either an appropriate direction or speed, Tish, an experienced dancer whose bored amusement could not be concealed beneath her professional courtesy, told me simply to "feel the music" and do whatever it said. I looked at her blankly, feeling hopelessly bewildered. Then I responded to deeper feelings than the music produced and excused myself. I left the room with clear direction and considerable speed and, with a wisdom born of shame, never returned for the two remaining lessons.

I did, however, escort Rachael to the campus event. And we danced. Not well—the toes of her shoes got a bit scuffed—but we moved across the dance floor together with my arms properly arranged. And I led, often into other couples and once, despite her whispered suggestions, into a table; but I led. The evening was an awkward success.

Learning how headship and submission actually work in a marriage is sometimes as clumsy as an inexperienced teenager learning to dance. There are rules to follow, there are roles that lay out the steps to take, but neither rules nor roles creates the awareness of rhythm that makes for good dancing.

There is a rhythm in relationship, a rhythm that can only be heard as the great truths about God are played over and over again. Increasingly we recognize what they mean and embrace them as true: truths about his holiness and our sinfulness, about his yearning for relationship with us and the length to which he went to satisfy those yearnings; truths about how he has made us, and his good purposes for us; truths about his indwelling, which means I live, yet not I, but Christ lives in me (Gal. 2:20).

Perhaps there is no more important truth for us to ponder than the fact that we are somehow like God, that we bear his image. And as we reflect on the wonder of all that it means to bear his image, the Scriptures quickly require us to notice another fact, that God has made us as men and women. There is a rhythm to the truth about our sexuality that must not be missed, a rhythm that when heard will move us in clear directions.

One theologian put the matter this way: "A person exists only as a man or woman. A person can never deny his maleness or her femaleness. A person does not just have a male or female body, he is a man and she is a woman. Sex is therefore not just one personal characteristic among others, but *a mode of being which determines one's whole life*"[3] (emphasis mine).

Our sexuality is expressed in all that we do. God's design is the music, and when we understand it and accept it with joy we begin to feel the rhythm of sexuality in our souls. Headship and submission represent masculine and feminine movements in the dance of relationship. They cannot be properly understood apart from realizing that, in marriage, headship is what a man does when he is living as a godly man, and submission is what a woman does when she is living as a godly woman. Headship and submission therefore are neither rules to follow nor roles that demand conformity. Rather, they are mature and loving expressions of our distinctive sexuality in the marriage relationship.

Headship and submission, when defined as opportunities to uniquely give to our spouses what they long to receive, become the route to enjoying the difference between men and women.

The differences are real and deep. Men are designed to enter their worlds of people and responsibilities with the confident and unthreatened strength of an advocate. Women are designed to invite other people into a nonmanipulative attachment that encourages the enjoyment of intimate relationship.

For all of us, the disease of justified selfishness is the central obstacle to developing good marriages and friendships. Success in life is measured by the quality of relationship we offer to our mates, children, parents, and friends. Do people in our circles feel loved and respected by us? Do we experience the joy of freely and eagerly giving what we have for the sake of another? If not, then the path to change begins with a hard look at our self-centeredness and at the wounds in our hearts that we use to justify the demand that others treat us well.

As repentance occurs, the path continues with an exploration of who we are as men and women. When we learn to warmly give what our sexual identity equips us to give to bless the masculine or feminine heart of our mate, then we will become men and women who enjoy the difference.

# Notes

## Introduction

[1]Ann Landers, *Los Angeles Times* (Friday, July 13, 1990): sec. E. Permission granted by Ann Landers and Creators Syndicate.

[2]Ann Landers, *Grand Rapids Press* (Thursday, September 20, 1990): sec. D.

## Chapter 5: Change is Possible

[1]"Natural Men in a Dreadful Condition," *Select Works of Jonathan Edwards, Vol. I*, ed. Ian Murray (The Banner of Truth Trust, 1965).

## Chapter 6: Celebrating Forgiveness

[1]D. Broughton Knox, *The Everlasting God* (Hertfordshire, England: Evangelical Press, 1982), 51, 52.

[2]I am indebted to Dr. Knox for these observations. See *The Everlasting God*, pp. 51—55.

[3]Emil Brunner, quoted in John Stott, *The Cross of Christ*, p. 88.

[4]See *Inside Out* (Colorado Springs, Colorado: NavPress, 1988) for a full discussion of how self-centered agendas develop.

## Chapter 7: A Tough Question

[1]J. I. Packer, "Understanding the Differences" in *Women, Authority, and the Bible*, edited by Alvers Mickelsen (Downers Grove: IVP, 1986), 298—99.

## Chapter 8: Is There Really a Difference?

[1]John Piper, *What's the Difference? Manhood and Womanhood Defined According to the Bible* (Westchester, Ill.: Crossway Books, 1990), ix.

[2]Ibid., 49.

[3]Carol Gilligan, *In a Different Voice* (Boston: Harvard University Press, 1982).

[4]Quoted in D. Bloesch, *Freedom for Obedience* (San Francisco: Harper & Row, 1987), 16.

## Chapter 9: Masculinity and Femininity

[1]See an article by John White entitled "AIDS, Judgment, and Blessing" in *Themelios*, Vol. 15, N. 2 (Jan/Feb 1990), 60–63. Contact IFES Link, 6400 Schroeder Rd., P.O. Box 7895, Madison, Wisconsin 53707-7895 for information about the journal.

[2]Read the story of Peter's gift to the lame beggar in Acts 3:1–10 as illustration of the point.

[3]Carol Gilligan, *In a Different Voice* (Boston: Harvard University Press, 1982), 159, 160.

[4]Ibid., 163.

## Chapter 10: Unique Ways to Freely Love

[1]John Piper, *What's the Difference? Manhood and Womanhood Defined According to the Bible* (Westchester, Ill.: Crossway Books, 1990), 16.

[2]Statement of position of *Men, Women and Biblical Equality*, published by Christians for Biblical Equality, 2830 Lower 138th St., Rosemount, Minnesota 55008.

[3]Piper, *What's the Difference?*, 19.

[4]Ibid.

[5]Paper by Christians for Biblical Equality.

## Chapter 12: Enjoying the Difference

[1]Quoted in Werner Neuer, *Man and Woman in Christian Perspective*, tr. by Gordon Wenham (London: Hodden and Stoughton, 1990), 127.

[2]John Piper, *What's the Difference? Manhood and Womanhood Defined According to the Bible* (Westchester, Ill.: Crossway Books, 1990), 34.

[3]Quoted in Werner Neuer, p. 127.